THE
SICILY
COOKBOOK

THE
SICILY
COOKBOOK

Authentic recipes from
a Mediterranean island

CETTINA VICENZINO

CONTENTS

INTRODUCTION

Our island has three corners. It has three oceans — the Tyrrhenian, Ionian, and Mediterranean — and a coat of arms with three legs (the Trinacria, see below). We have three tribes of ancestors — the Sicani, Elymians, and Sicels — and three mountain ranges — Monti Peloritani, Nebrodi, and Madonie — which are a continuation of the Apennines. The Italian mainland is just three kilometres (two miles) away, across the narrowest point of the strait of Messina. Our volcano is roughly 3,330m (11,000ft) high and our cuisine has three main influences: *cucina povera*, *cibo di strada*, and *cucina dei Monsù* (more of which later). Our *fava larga*, the longest beans in Italy, are traditionally harvested with a three-pronged fork. And there are three products that no Sicilian cook can do without: olive oil, salt, and wheat. My mother, who embodies Sicily for me, was born on the third of the month. All good things about our island come in threes. Between black and white there is a third realm of amazing and magical colour. And that's where you'll find Sicily.

Just a decade ago, it wasn't easy to publish a cookbook about Sicily. Back then, Italy was widely regarded overseas as consisting primarily of Tuscany, plus a few of the larger, more glamorous cities, such as Venice, Milan, and Rome. When I presented my Sicilian cookbook to publishers, the consensus was that I should simply make it about Italian food. Nobody would be interested in Sicily, I was told, and it didn't really matter whether the recipes were Italian or Sicilian. I was not to be persuaded, and wrote and published my first book on Sicily regardless. Italy and Sicily are worlds apart, separated by almost 4,000 years of history. One of my favourite Sicilian chefs loves to tell his Italian colleagues that the islanders were already drinking from glasses, eating from plates, and going to the theatre while the Italians were still clambering about in the trees. Unsurprisingly, the Italians themselves tell exactly the same story, but with the roles reversed…

What is indisputable is that Sicily has always been a trading centre and a melting pot for lots of different cultures, thanks largely to its strategic position in the Mediterranean. Sicily gathered new foods, knowledge, and architecture from visitors and invaders alike and — inevitably — suffered a certain amount of destruction too. The island has undergone relentless transformations and, from the ruin caused by each new regime, something new emerged. In this way, one of the most diverse cultural environments in Europe developed.

This process continued unabated until the 19th century, then stopped at a time more or less coinciding with the unification of Italy. From then on, a weakened Sicily was afflicted by a serious disease: the Mafia. But this should not be confused with Sicilian culture. "Our identity is not the Mafia. The Mafia has just perverted it," says Leoluca Orlando, the mayor of Palermo, the island's capital city.

A lot has changed in the decade since I published my first Sicilian cookbook, and not just in the recipe book business — in which Sicilian food and culture is now considered a worthy subject for close study — but on the island itself.

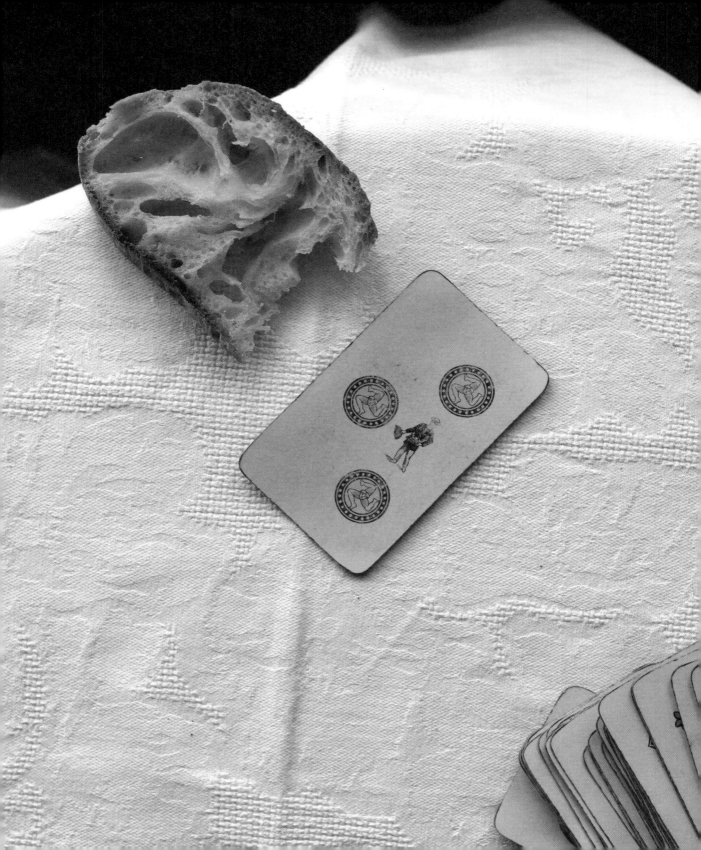

Much of this can be credited to the mayor of Palermo, who has successfully persuaded islanders that they can reclaim their country through a renewed appreciation of its true culture. People are increasingly rediscovering their roots, and so liberating themselves from the Hollywood folklore that is obsessed with the Mafia and threatens to infect the world's view of the island.

A true scholar of Sicily knows that the island's culture – the history of its chefs, food producers, culinary innovators, and restaurant owners – goes back much further than the 160 years that has captivated Hollywood. Now that their history and true origins are being properly researched, we often find links back to the Sicani, the Elymians, and the Sicels, the original inhabitants of Sicily, who lived here even before the first Greek colonization in the eighth century BCE. The Sicani, who are thought to be Iberian in origin, inhabited central Sicily. The Elymians lived in the western region and are believed to have come from Troy, which is probably in present-day Turkey. The east of the island was settled by the Sicels, who historians think migrated from the Italian mainland, and after whom Sicily was ultimately named. (I deliberately describe this migrant status as hypothetical, because the Sicani refer to themselves in ancient texts as an indigenous people.)

In the meantime, there are certainly plenty of native foods that are being rediscovered and cherished once more in Sicily. Ancient strains of grain are being used again to make pasta, bread, and traditionally brewed beers. Sicilian pulses that were dying out have been resurrected and grown on a large scale once more, and there is a push to protect the island's sesame from commercial genetic modification. Indigenous vines are being revived, rare ancient breeds of livestock are being farmed, while forgotten varieties of cheese – such as Tuma Persa made by Salvatore Passalacqua from Castronovo di Sicilia – are enjoying a resurgence. Not to mention the renewed appreciation of *manna*, the medicinal white juice of the ash tree, which is being extracted and used as a sweetener in Sicilian *pasticcerie*.

Idealists and artisans are driving this new Sicilian love of its original culture, and ever-increasing numbers of the island's inhabitants are joining them. There is street art all over the place, with murals and installations springing up everywhere. But this reacquaintance with the past does not reveal a desire to escape the vicissitudes of the present day, or of the future. On the contrary, modern Sicilians have a clear vision for themselves and their future, as articulated so beautifully by the Amore family (see p130).

The recipes in this book are a blend of the three ancient Sicilian cuisines: *cucina dei Monsù*, *cibo di strada*, and *cucina povera*. (For more detail, see p86, p112, and p130.) Sicilian cooking also combines the best aspects of Italian and North African cuisines and takes advantage of other food influences from its many conquerors. This book contains reworkings of typical Sicilian dishes as well as traditional recipes, such as the renowned *pasta alla Norma*, which is – sadly – seldom made authentically, despite its global popularity (see p23).

Italian cookbooks usually begin with antipasti. But Sicilian cuisine doesn't really include this course. Everything that is served as antipasto in Sicily today was originally a side dish, or, during the harsher times of the island's history, the only food served. That is why the largest chapter is Piatto unico (see pp84–139). Anything which could be a side dish or a snack – and thus is also suitable as an antipasto – can be found in the Intermezzi chapter (see pp.140–177). Many of the products mentioned in the book are now available in supermarkets, such as Sicilian

pecorino, *scamorza affumicata*, Sicilian artichokes, and whole rabbits. Others, such as wild fennel, require a bit of luck to track down, but at least this ingredient can be replaced by a combination of fresh dill and soaked fennel seeds. But that's fine, because a cookbook is not supposed to be a substitute for a country and its flavours. What it can do is evoke a cooking culture and stimulate a curiosity to learn more about it. And that is my aim.

So, if you are looking for a Sicilian cookbook that only contains lots of recipes, this isn't the book for you. However, if you want to find out more about Sicilian culture, if you are curious about the people who live there, then this is the perfect choice.

I hope you really enjoy reading my book, which has become as much a part of me as Sicily.

Yours,

Cettina Vicenzino

SICILY:
A CULTURAL GUIDE

Sicily is the largest island in the Mediterranean. It covers an area of 25,832sq km (9,974sq m), making it almost as big as Belgium. More than 5 million people live in Sicily. The capital, Palermo, has more than 1.25 million inhabitants, while second city Catania is home to more than 1.1 million people.

Constant invasions: the rulers of Sicily

During ancient times, the sophisticated Sicani, Elymian, and Sicel tribes lived peacefully in different parts of the island. The first trading posts were established by the Phoenicians in the west of the island. In the eighth century BCE the first Greek colony was established, and, while the Greeks enriched the island with a new culture and economy, they also sought to oust the indigenous people.

In 210 BCE the Romans arrived, making Sicily the breadbasket of Rome and, in the process, destroying almost all its forests. In the fifth century CE, the Vandals and Ostrogoths plundered the island, then, from 535, Sicily became part of Byzantium for 300 years.

The Arabs conquered Sicily in 827, rebuilt it, and let it flourish. Their tolerance towards all the other religions on the island made them popular with the people.

In 1061 the Normans conquered Sicily and, in 1194, they were followed by the Hohenstaufen dynasty, originally from Germany. The French Anjou kings and the Spanish House of Aragon that followed them were oppressive regimes, that neglected the island.

A devastating volcanic eruption occurred at Mount Etna in 1669 and an equally destructive earthquake brought further anguish in 1693. (Many areas that were destroyed in the south-east region of the island were rebuilt in Sicilian Baroque style, and were declared a world heritage site by UNESCO in 2002.)

From 1713 to 1720 the island was ruled by the dukes of Savoy and Piedmont, from 1720 to 1735 the Austrian Habsburgs took over, and, from 1735 to 1860, it was the turn of the Spanish Bourbons. None of these three were popular with the people of the island. In 1816, Sicily was united with Naples to form the Kingdom of Sicily. Unification with Italy came in 1861 and, sadly, Sicily was once again allowed to fall into a state of neglect. Up until the 20th century, there was a massive wave of emigration.

In 1946, Sicily became an autonomous region with its own parliament. In 1986, the largest trial against organized crime took place, and, in 2018, Italy chose Palermo as the country's Capital of Culture.

Sicilian generosity

Despite their long history of exploitation, most Sicilians are exceptionally generous and will give even when they have nothing. If you visit Sicily, please don't take advantage of this trait; all too often over the course of history, strangers have taken from the islanders without giving back. Even if someone absolutely refuses to accept money, Sicilians will still find a charming way of paying recompense, returning a favour in some other manner. Try to do the same.

Getting around

Being carless, I tested out buses, ferries, and trains all over the island. Even without a car, as a woman travelling alone, there is lots of great public transport, as well as private bus companies that are great value and punctual.

pistacchi ~ pinoli

mandorle · arancia rossa

ficu.

primo sale · belicino · coffanetto

olive

lenticchie

fave

pomodoro cuore di bue

melanzane

arancini

cassata

capra girgentana

cavolfiore viola

pane mafalda

suino nero dei nebrodi

sarde

Cacio cavallo

cannoli

finocchietto

pesce spada

spatola

provola

capperi

fichi d'india

triglie

grillo

nero d'avola

fichi

limone cedro

acciughe

gelsi

ricci di mare

polipo

maccheroni ~ aneletti

LA MELANZANA

If you ask a Sicilian for their favourite dishes containing aubergines, you'll be there for some time listening to the reply. Aubergines feature in many of the island's most famous recipes, from *caponata di melanzane*, the sweet-sour salad, to succulent stuffed *melanzane ripiene*. Perhaps you'll prefer luscious *melanzane alla parmigiana*, layered with melting cheese, or a comforting *pasta alla Norma*. From casseroles, to pickled under oil, the aubergine is king in Sicily.

A Sicilian kitchen without an aubergine is unthinkable. You might almost believe the vegetable was a native of Sicily, given how often it is used in the island's recipes.

The most widespread technique for preparing aubergines around the world is probably as stuffed aubergine halves, or perhaps served as a smoky puréed aubergine dip (*baba ganoush*). You might find it sliced, griddled, and served in a salad. But that's about it. The Sicilians, meanwhile, have more than 80 recipes for this vegetable.

The aubergine is a master of versatility, with a fabulous savoury-yet-sweet flavour. It can be used as a soft purée, or as a firm meat substitute cooked in the same way as a pork chop (*alla cotoletta*). Contemporary Sicilian cooks experiment with it in all sorts of ways. Alongside risotto balls *arancini alla Norma*, inspired by the famous *pasta alla Norma*, you will also find more idiosyncratic creations, especially among the island's restaurant menus. In his restaurant La Madia in Licata, for instance, the two Michelin-starred chef Pino Cuttaia rustles up tubes made from perlina aubergines (see p21), wrapped in crispy pasta, with cherry tomatoes and Ragusano cheese. Head chef Roberto Toro from the Belmond Grand Hotel Timeo in Taormina offers an interesting gnocchi made from aubergines, rather than the traditional potatoes, in a tomato sauce.

And yet the aubergine doesn't even come from Sicily, originating instead in south-east Asia, India, and China. It was the Arabs who introduced it to Europe and, in the late 14th century, it caught the attention of the Sicilians for the first time, being grown around the island and referred to by one of Sicily's Carmelite orders of monks in their medicinal botanical survey.

However, the aubergine was initially a failure on the island, due to the fact that the people were prone to dying after eating it raw! That is how it acquired its vernacular name *mela non sana*, or "unhealthy apple", which over the years has become *melanzana*. Along with other members of the nightshade family, such as potatoes, aubergine contains the toxin solanine, which is why it must not be eaten raw.

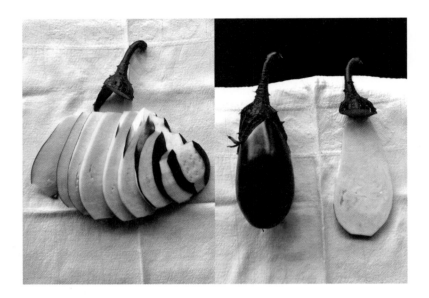

What *has* changed over time is the vegetable's bitterness, which is barely – if at all – perceptible in newer varieties. In old cookbooks, readers were always instructed to sprinkle aubergines with salt before cooking, to extract their bitter juices by osmosis. Nowadays, this process is only necessary if you want to avoid the vegetable soaking up too much oil when you fry it. (Otherwise, aubergines are notorious for mopping up oil like sponges.) However, through osmosis, aubergines not only lose water, but also some minerals. There are varieties that naturally absorb less oil and so are better for any dishes that require the aubergine to be fried. For these recipes, look around for the *nera di Palermo* or the *sciacchitana* (see right), both older varieties.

There is an aubergine best suited to every recipe. The different varieties can be categorized into three basic shapes: round, oval, and cylindrical. Since aubergines turn brown when ripe – and the flesh inside becomes fibrous, too – you might be surprised to learn that they are harvested and eaten while still unripe.

Here is a summary of the types available in Sicily, the first five of which are traditional Sicilian varieties:

-01- Melanzana ovale nera
Very versatile. Try it cubed in sauces or baked dishes, fried, stuffed, for *involtini*, or preserved in oil.

-02- Melanzana nera di Palermo
This absorbs little oil, so is ideal for frying, and is firm with few seeds. Good in *parmigiana*, stuffed, or cubed.

-03- Melanzana Baffa "Black Beauty"
An aubergine with few seeds and firm flesh, best for frying or baking, roasting, or preserving in oil.

-04- Melanzana sciacchitana nera
Widely available, this absorbs little oil, so is ideal for sautéing, deep-frying, or use in stuffed aubergine recipes.

-05- Melanzana nera mezza lunga
Excellent for frying, to be preserved in oil, for *involtini*, or cubed in aubergine sauces.

-06- Melanzana violetta seta
Delicate and very sweet. Best for frying, for *parmigiana*, *pasta alla Norma*, baked dishes, or preserving in oil.

-07- Melanzana mini perlina
This widely available variety is compact, with flesh that contains little water, so it does not absorb much oil. It is excellent cooked whole, or fried in cubes, for baked dishes, *involtini*, or *caponata*.

-08- Melanzana zebrina viola
A fine flavour and very sweet, with striped skin. For *parmigiana*, *caponata*, for baked dishes, stuffed, or fried.

-09- Melanzana bianca
With few seeds and an edible white skin, this is good for frying, baking, and for typical recipes such as *parmigiana*, *caponata*, *involtini*, and stuffed dishes.

-10- Melanzana violetta Messinese
A widely available variety, delicate and very sweet. Excellent for frying, for *pasta alla Norma,* and *parmigiana*.

-11- Melanzana tonda violetta prosperosa
A subtle and rounded flavour, for baked dishes, or frying.

-12- Melanzana violetta Palermitana
Like its cousins above, delicate and sweet. Suitable for frying and roasting, and excellent for *parmigiana*, *pasta alla Norma*, or for preserving in oil.

-13- Melanzana violetta zuccherina
A fine flavour and, as the name suggests, full of natural sugars. Try it chopped into aubergine sauces, for succulent baked dishes, or fried, stuffed, or for the classics *involtini* and *parmigiana*.

-14- Melanzana tonda violetta bella Vittoria
Last but not least, this aubergine is delicate and very sweet. Good cubed for pasta sauce, baked, fried, roasted, stuffed, for *involtini*, or *parmigiana*.

PASTA ALLA NORMA

If there is a pasta dish which best represents Sicily, it is surely *pasta alla Norma* (see pp24–25). This vegetarian summer recipe, originally from Catania, owes its appeal to just a few ingredients, which have to be of the finest quality. Most importantly, the way in which it is assembled is vital to its success.

The comparison of an aubergine pasta dish with Bellini's opera *Norma* was supposedly first made by Nino Martoglio, a poet, playwright, and gourmet from Catania, the home of the recipe. He is meant to have exclaimed, *"Chista è 'na vera Norma!"* ("That is a real Norma!"), after eating his first forkful.

If you have eaten *pasta alla Norma* outside Italy, you may well wonder what a rather ordinary dish made with short macaroni and bite-sized pieces of aubergine – chopped as though the cook was in a hurry – has to do with such an esteemed opera. The answer is nothing, because a dish made with macaroni and chopped aubergine is no *Norma*, but simply the household staple *pasta con le melanzane*. Though even in that humble dish, the aubergine shouldn't be chopped. And, if we are being especially strict, macaroni with chopped aubergine should always be made with homemade macaroni.

You may have come across a more elaborate dish made with homemade cavatelli pasta, mozzarella, tomatoes, aubergines, *caciocavallo* or *ricotta salata* cheese, and basil. However, this is no *Norma* either, but a *cavatelli al cartoccio* from the region around Agrigento.

A genuine *Norma* must be composed like an opera in three acts. What is lacking from the widely available fast-food version with its macaroni and chopped aubergine is this process of arrangement, the careful assembly and compilation. And this can only be achieved if you serve it on not one plate, but three.

An authentic *Norma* has one plate with spaghetti, tomato sauce, and aubergine strips torn by hand. A second plate holds fried slices of aubergine. The last plate contains grated *ricotta salata* (salted ricotta).

Each person grabs one of the plates from the table before passing it on. You take sliced aubergine, place as many pieces as you want on your pasta, then sprinkle with ricotta. Since short pasta pieces don't go well with large discs of aubergine, or even aubergine strips, it is essential to use spaghetti. (This is also far more elegant and befitting a dish named after an opera, as you can twirl them around your fork, rather than having to stab them as you do with macaroni.) It is a mystery to me why the inauthentic version with its macaroni and chopped pieces of aubergine has become so widespread around the world.

Luckily, I have never yet been served *pasta alla Norma* with macaroni and chopped aubergine in the province of Catania. Which is not to say that this inferior version cannot be found in Catania, too. More's the pity…

Pasta with tomato, aubergines, and ricotta salata

Pasta alla Norma e ricotta salata

700g (1lb 9oz) aubergines,
   ideally *nera di Palermo*
   (see p20), though regular
   aubergines are fine
coarse sea salt
1kg (2¼lb) sweet, ripe
   cherry tomatoes
extra virgin olive oil
   (I use Tonda Iblea)
2 garlic cloves, ideally pink
   garlic, finely sliced
sea salt
2 handfuls of basil leaves,
   half roughly shredded
chilli flakes
320g (11oz) spaghetti
80g (2¾oz) *ricotta salata*,
   or pecorino cheese,
   finely grated

Remove the stems from the aubergines, cut them lengthways into 5–7mm- (¼in-) thick slices, sprinkle on both sides with coarse sea salt, and place in a sieve over the kitchen sink. Set aside for 30 minutes to draw out the water.

Meanwhile, remove and discard the stalks from the tomatoes and place in a large bowl. Pour over boiling water from the kettle to just cover and leave for 30 seconds, then drain. The skins should slip off. Remove the skins and finely chop the flesh.

Brush the salt off the aubergine slices and dab them dry, pressing firmly. Heat 5–6 tbsp olive oil in a large, deep saucepan and cook the garlic until it gets a bit of colour, but don't let it burn. Then stir in the tomatoes, add some sea salt, stir in the shredded basil, season with chilli flakes, and simmer gently until the sauce has thickened slightly.

Heat about 1cm (½in) of olive oil in a frying pan over a medium heat. Fry the aubergine slices – in batches so as not to crowd the pan – in the hot oil until golden. Drain on kitchen paper. Tear 4 slices into strips by hand and set everything aside to keep warm.

Fill a large saucepan with plenty of water and place over a high heat. When it comes to the boil, sprinkle in coarse sea salt and cook the spaghetti until *al dente* (usually 1 minute less than the time stated on the packet). Drain the pasta, return it to the pan, then mix well with the tomato sauce and the torn strips of aubergine.

Arrange the pasta on a serving dish and scatter with the remaining basil leaves. Put the sautéed whole aubergine slices on a second serving dish, and the grated cheese on a third, then serve.

Drawing out the water: today's aubergine varieties don't usually need to have their juices extracted to remove bitterness (see p20). The reason we do it here is to avoid the slices soaking up too much oil. If you would prefer to skip this step, you will use more oil when frying, but this can mostly be removed by laying the slices on kitchen paper. In any case, to prepare a genuine *Norma*, you should be generous with the olive oil.

Pasta towers with meat sauce and aubergines

Sformatini di anelletti

For the meat sauce

1 long, narrow aubergine, ideally *mezza lunga* (see p20), though regular aubergines are fine

coarse sea salt

extra virgin olive oil (I use Tonda Iblea)

130g (4½oz) Sicilian sausages, or coarsely minced pork

1 garlic clove, ideally pink garlic, finely chopped

20g (¾oz) pancetta, finely chopped

150g (5½oz) passata

½ tbsp tomato purée, or *strattù* (see p40)

sea salt

chilli flakes

basil leaves, roughly shredded, plus small leaves, to serve

For the pasta towers

160g (5¾oz) anelletti or other short pasta

4 tbsp finely grated pecorino cheese

80g (2¾oz) provolone cheese, sliced into rounds

2 medium hard-boiled eggs, peeled and sliced

2 cherry tomatoes

2 tbsp dried breadcrumbs, or *mollica secca* (see p30)

extra virgin olive oil

2 tbsp finely grated *ricotta salata* cheese

Usually, Sicilian anelletti pasta hoops are used for this recipe, but rigatoni, macaroni, or other small pasta shapes work just as well (see p53). You can double the quantities for this recipe and make a large tower in a round cake tin, if you prefer. If you do this, line the tin with the fried slices of aubergine and fill with the pasta. After cooking, carefully turn the dish out of the tin.

Remove the stem of the aubergine, slice widthways into 12 slices roughly 1cm (½in) thick, place in a sieve, sprinkle with coarse sea salt and set aside for 30 minutes. Heat about 1cm (½in) of olive oil in a frying pan over a medium heat, then sauté the slices – in batches so as not to crowd the pan – until golden. Drain on kitchen paper.

Meanwhile, heat 1 tbsp olive oil in another pan. Squeeze the sausagemeat out of its skin, if using. Gently fry the garlic, pancetta, and sausagemeat or minced pork. Pour in the passata. Mix the tomato purée or *strattù* with 4 tbsp of water and stir this in, too. Season to taste with salt and chilli flakes, scatter over the shredded basil, and simmer until the meat is cooked.

Fill a large saucepan with plenty of water and place over a high heat. When it comes to the boil, sprinkle in coarse sea salt and cook the pasta until almost *al dente* (1–2 minutes less than the time stated on the packet). Drain. Add the pasta to the meat sauce, then stir in the grated pecorino.

Preheat the oven to 180°C (350°F/ Gas 4). Line a baking tray with baking parchment and place on 4 metal rings, each 6cm (2½in) high and 7–8cm (3in) in diameter.

In each ring, place a slice of aubergine and spoon some of the pasta on top. Then add a slice of provolone and one-quarter of the egg slices and cover with a second slice of aubergine. Scoop in some more pasta and finish off with a final slice of aubergine.

Remove the stalks from the cherry tomatoes, chop finely and mix with the breadcrumbs. Scatter over the prepared ring moulds. Drizzle lightly with olive oil and bake in the centre of the oven for about 20 minutes.

Remove the cooked towers from the oven, leave to cool slightly, then carefully release from their moulds and serve immediately with *ricotta salata*, the small basil leaves, and a few drops of olive oil.

Pasta with sardines (rich & poor)

Pasta con le sarde (ricchi & poveri)

100g (3½oz) wild fennel, or
   the same amount of dill
   with 1 tbsp fennel seeds,
   soaked in water for
   20 minutes, then drained
coarse sea salt
extra virgin olive oil
10 fresh sardines, filleted
   (see p64), or ask your
   fishmonger to do this
1 onion, finely chopped
1 garlic clove, ideally pink
   garlic, finely chopped
4 anchovies in oil, drained
70ml (2½fl oz) dry white
   wine
20g (¾oz) tomato purée, or
   strattù (see p40)
30g (1oz) sultanas, soaked in
   warm water for 20 minutes,
   then drained
20g (¾oz) pine nuts, toasted
20g (¾oz) blanched almonds,
   toasted and roughly
   chopped
4–6g (⅛oz) saffron threads,
   plus a small pinch extra
sea salt
chilli flakes
300g (10oz) bucatini or
   spaghetti
80g (2¾oz) dried
   breadcrumbs, or
   mollica secca (see p30)

Poor islanders would often try to mimic the recipes served to Sicilian nobility. There's a dish called *pasta chi sárdi a mári* ("pasta with sardines that are still in the sea" – in other words, without any fish). And in *pasta chi sárdi russi* the saffron is replaced by *strattù*, tomato purée. The original *pasta con le sarde* doesn't contain any tomatoes at all, but my version is a combination of both the rich and poor recipes.

Set aside 5 sprigs of wild fennel, if using. Cook the rest for 5–8 minutes in a large saucepan of generously salted water. Drain and set aside the liquid. Dab the fennel dry and chop.

Meanwhile, heat some olive oil in a frying pan. Sauté 12 sardine fillets in the oil, flipping to cook both sides. They should not become too dark. Set aside to keep warm.

Heat 5–6 tbsp more olive oil in a large saucepan. Sauté the onion and garlic, then add the drained anchovies. As soon as they begin to disintegrate, deglaze the pan with the white wine. Let the alcohol evaporate slightly. Mix the tomato purée or *strattù* with 100ml (3½fl oz) of the fennel cooking water – or warm water, if you didn't use wild fennel – and stir this into the pan. Put the remaining 8 sardine fillets in the pan, then carefully mix in the sultanas, pine nuts, almonds, pre-cooked wild fennel, or dill and drained fennel seeds, and the 4–6g (⅛oz) saffron.

Season everything to taste with salt and chilli flakes. Simmer for a further 10–12 minutes.

Meanwhile, return the remaining fennel water to the boil, if using, otherwise fill a large saucepan with plenty of water and place over a high heat. When it comes to the boil, sprinkle in coarse sea salt and the remaining small pinch of saffron threads and cook the spaghetti until *al dente* (usually 1 minute less than the time stated on the packet).

Drain the pasta and combine with the sauce. Divide between 4 plates, arrange 3 of the reserved sardine fillets on each portion, sprinkle with breadcrumbs, and garnish with a sprig of wild fennel, if using, or dill. Drizzle with olive oil and serve.

This dish actually consists of one *primo* (the pasta) and one *secondo* (the fish), so it could also be served as a *piatto unico* (from p84).

The mayor of Palermo's favourite pasta

Pasta alla Leoluca

50g (2³/₄oz) anchovies
preserved in oil
100g (3¹/₂oz) dried
breadcrumbs, or *mollica
secca* (see right)
sugar
sea salt
6 tbsp extra virgin olive
oil, plus extra for cooking
the breadcrumbs
coarse sea salt
250g (9oz) bucatini or
spaghetti
1 garlic clove, finely
chopped
25g (scant 1oz) pine nuts
50g (2³/₄oz) sultanas, soaked
in warm water for 20
minutes, then drained
3 tbsp tomato purée, or
strattù (see p40)

More than a decade ago, mayor Leoluca Orlando prepared this dish on television, a quick version of *pasta con le sarde* (see p29). The expensive saffron in that recipe is replaced in this version by the island's homemade tomato purée, *strattù* (see p40). There are no sardines or wild fennel in this dish.

Drain the anchovies and slice each in half lengthways.

Mix the breadcrumbs with a little sugar and a pinch of salt.

Heat some olive oil in a frying pan over a medium heat and toast the breadcrumbs in the oil. Scrape the crumbs into a bowl.

Fill a large saucepan with plenty of water and place over a high heat. When it comes to the boil, sprinkle in coarse sea salt and cook the bucatini until *al dente* (usually 1 minute less than the time stated on the packet).

Meanwhile, heat the 6 tbsp of olive oil in the frying pan and sauté the anchovies and garlic until the fish starts to melt and the garlic begins to colour (don't let it burn). Add the pine nuts and drained sultanas and continue to cook briefly. Stir 2 tbsp of water into the tomato purée or *strattù*, mix this into the sauce, and let everything simmer gently.

Drain the bucatini and combine with the sauce, season to taste with salt if desired, and serve scattered with the fried breadcrumbs.

Mollica: the poor in Sicily traditionally cooked with *mollica* (the ground crumbs from stale bread). Sometimes this was mixed with olive oil and toasted – as in this recipe – as a substitute for expensive pecorino cheese. There's a difference between *mollica fresca*, in which only the crumb of the loaf is used, and *mollica secca*, which includes the crust.

Serves 4
Prep 30 mins

Pasta carriage-style

Pasta alla carrettiera

500g (1lb 2oz) cherry
   tomatoes
2 large garlic cloves
2 handfuls of basil leaves
extra virgin olive oil
   (I use Tonda Iblea)
sea salt
chilli flakes
coarse sea salt
320g (11oz) ruote,
   or spaghetti
80g (2³/₄oz) pecorino cheese,
   finely grated

There are as many variations of this dish as there are mysteries about it. The story goes that it was created by the carriage drivers who used to travel the island and didn't want to be deprived of their pasta, and thus used just a few ingredients that keep well. So the fact that fresh tomatoes seem to have been used in the original recipe is rather puzzling. Having said this, there are popular versions of this dish in Sicily which have the same name but don't contain any fresh ingredients at all. You will also come across recipes with the same ingredients, but in which they are cooked rather than used raw. Originally, *pasta alla carrettiera* was made with raw ingredients; only the pasta was cooked. As a rule, spaghetti is used but, in my opinion, wagon wheel-shaped ruote pasta works beautifully, especially given the name of the recipe.

Remove and discard the stalks from the tomatoes and place in a large bowl. Pour over boiling water from the kettle to just cover and leave for 30 seconds, then drain. The skins should slip off. Remove the skins, finely chop the flesh, and place in a bowl.

Smash one of the garlic cloves (leaving it intact) and slice the other into slivers. Mix both of these with the tomatoes. Roughly tear the basil and mix into the tomatoes with a generous 2 tbsp olive oil. Season to taste with salt and chilli and leave to infuse for 15 minutes.

Fill a large saucepan with plenty of water and place over a high heat. When it comes to the boil, sprinkle in coarse sea salt and cook the pasta until *al dente* (usually 1 minute less than the time stated on the packet).

Drain the pasta. Remove the smashed garlic clove from the sauce, discard, then add the pasta to the sauce. Sprinkle over half the cheese and mix thoroughly. Divide between plates, sprinkle over the remaining cheese, drizzle with a dash of oil, and serve.

Pasta with spring vegetables, sun-dried tomatoes, and ricotta

Pasta u pitaggiu

4 small artichokes, ideally
    from Sicily
1 organic lemon
coarse sea salt
320g (11oz) short pasta, such
    as cataneselle, sedani, or
    short macaroni (see p53)
extra virgin olive oil
4 spring onions with large
    bulbs (around 100g/3½oz
    in total), white parts
    only, sliced
1kg (2lb 4oz) broad beans,
    podded, blanched, and
    removed from their skins
400g (14oz) fresh peas,
    podded
16 sun-dried cherry
    tomatoes, or 12 regular
    sun-dried tomatoes, in oil
1–2 tbsp finely chopped mint
    leaves, plus whole leaves,
    to serve
4 tbsp white wine vinegar
1 tbsp sugar
sea salt
chilli flakes
4 tbsp ricotta cheese

This vegetable stew originates from Castrofilippo in the province of Agrigento. It is often made as a side dish for Sicilian sausages, or combined with rice, and it also works beautifully in a fritatta. My version is a pasta sauce that includes tomatoes, ricotta, and short pasta *all'agrodolce* (sweet-sour). In Sicily, they would use a spiny variety of artichokes from Menfi (*carciofi spinosi*).

Prepare the artichokes (see right).

Fill a large saucepan with plenty of water and place over a high heat. When it comes to the boil, sprinkle in coarse sea salt and cook the pasta until *al dente* (usually 1 minute less than the time stated on the packet). Retain some of the cooking water when you drain the pasta.

Meanwhile, heat some olive oil in a sauté pan over a medium–low heat. Sauté the onions. Gently fry the artichokes in the pan, then add the beans and peas and cook briefly. Next stir in the tomatoes and mint and braise for 3–5 minutes. Now stir together 80ml (2½fl oz) of water, the vinegar, and sugar. Pour this in and season with salt and chilli. Cover and leave to braise for 5 minutes.

Mix the vegetables with the pasta and some of the cooking water. Add a couple of dollops of ricotta to the pasta on each plate, drizzle with a bit of olive oil and scatter over the mint leaves.

Preparing the artichokes:

Squeeze the lemon, then mix the juice with water in a large bowl.

For large artichokes, trim the stalk down to 3cm (1¼in), peeling several layers off the very woody section. For young artichokes, trim the stalk by one-third and peel in a similar manner. Remove plenty of the outermost leaves until almost all that is left is the base. Use a knife to expose the outer edge of the artichoke base, cutting off any remaining leaf sections around the base as you do so.

Slice the artichokes in half lengthways and scrape out the stringy fibres in the centre with the tip of the knife or a teaspoon. (Young artichokes don't have these, and can be used whole.)

Put the prepared artichokes into the bowl with the lemon water until ready to use, to prevent them from turning brown.

ELVIRA

If you glance up from the Valley of the Temples towards
the centre of Agrigento, the view is not especially
inviting. But if you knew what is concealed behind the
box-shaped new buildings, you could imagine these
apartment blocks as powerful guardians, protecting
the magnificent heart of the old town by keeping it
secret so it doesn't suffer a fresh assault.

This has been a recurring theme in the history of
Agrigento, which was constantly being renamed depending
on who ruled it at the time. The Greeks gave the town the
name Akragas, the Romans called it Agrigentum, the Arabs
coined the name Kerkent, while the Normans referred to
the place as Girgenti. From 1927 onwards, during the
fascist regime, the Italian name Agrigento was adopted
and continues to be used today.

Visitors who aren't put off by the new buildings and who
approach the high ground on which the town is situated
find a stunning and vibrant historical centre. There are
few hotels (virtually none), but the old town is brimming
with smaller bed-and-breakfast options.

Visitors to Agrigento are spoilt for choice: an amazing number of guest houses are crammed into this little town. In every pretty, winding alleyway and passage you will find at least one equally attractive place to stay. And sometimes your luck is in and you make exactly the right choice. In which case, you may end up at Elvira's place: Camere a Sud.

Elvira opened her bed-and-breakfast in 2004, and it was quite a rarity at the time. She had studied law and communication and, after university, lived and worked for two years in Rome. But, along with her husband, she decided to return home. "We Sicilians, if we all leave the island, nothing will grow here any more. So I thought – even if it's just a small contribution – I could do my bit to help. I wanted to come back."

Before she opened Camere a Sud there were absolutely no guest houses in Agrigento. Now the place is full of them, and that's fantastic because this is how a town can gain new life. But when Elvira started her business, it was unusual for a university graduate to take tourists into their own home. It was even regarded as slightly shocking, as the bed-and-breakfast is not an Italian concept. It was pretty much unknown and people did not know what to make of it.

Over time, Elvira began to write, inspired by all the exceptional guests she had got to know as a host. Her attitude to life also changed. Instead of believing that the universe revolved around herself, she began to realise that it revolves around other people. "We are all different, and these differences result in something that really fascinates me," she explains.

"So that's why I'm so interested in people and what it means to be human. My writing is almost like a kind of anthropological study, just for me. I started to document genuine stories, without using real names, about things that actually happened here in my bed-and-breakfast between check-in and check-out." Initially she published these stories on Facebook and, when she stopped posting them online, there was an immediate flood of complaints from her readers, who were already hooked on reading the tales.

There's always a positive twist to her accounts; no matter how tragic a situation might be, she will find something good. Some stories are ironic, others move you to tears.

Elvira told me, "I have to write down everything I know about an amazing person or situation straight away, otherwise the moment is lost and I forget the scintillating details. The whole world happens here." And I am suddenly reminded that one of the most important 20th century playwrights, Luigi Pirandello, who received the Nobel prize for literature in 1934, was born in Agrigento.

Before I leave, Elvira hands me another jar of the particularly fine pistachio cream which is always on offer at the breakfast buffet, and also a jar of her mother's tomato sauce. A typically generous gesture from this fabulous Agrigento host.

Makes six x 250ml
(9fl oz) jars
Prep 40 mins, plus
draining time

Elvira's mama's homemade raw tomato passata

Conserva di pomodori a crudo

2kg (4¹/₂lb) very ripe
    tomatoes, ideally San
    Marzano (you can also
    use sweet, ripe cherry
    tomatoes)
sea salt
basil leaves (optional)

Elvira just cannot eat any tomato sauce other than her mother's. Even as a child she adored it. First her mother would let the tomatoes dry in the sun so their water evaporated (even the shape of the tomatoes had to be right). Elvira's mama would then strain the tomatoes by hand. In late summer she would make enough to keep them supplied with passata throughout the winter. One of Elvira's mum's ingredients can't be bought: sunshine. So the tomatoes for this recipe have to be *really* ripe.

Discard the stalks from the tomatoes, chop into large chunks, and place in a sieve. Sprinkle with salt and leave to drain for about 1 hour. Strain the tomatoes to produce a purée, using a vegetable mill. If the sauce is too thin, place a fine sieve over a bowl, line it with a clean cotton or muslin cloth and pour in the sauce. Leave to drain until the sauce has achieved the desired consistency.

Rinse 6 screw-top jars in boiling hot water. Fill with passata up to about 2cm (¾in) below the rim. Place a large basil leaf on top of each (if you like), and seal the jar tight.

Place a clean tea towel in a large pan, then put in the jars. Place a second towel in between the jars to stop them rattling during the boiling process. Fill the pan two-thirds full with boiling water. Cover and return the water to the boil, then continue boiling for 20 minutes. Turn off the heat and leave the jars to cool in the pan.

Store the passata in a cool, dark place. If kept sealed, it will keep for 1 year. Once opened, store in the refrigerator and use within 5 days.

Strattù: another laborious task undertaken in summer by the village women was the production of Sicilian tomato purée, or *strattù*. During this period, a wonderful aroma would waft through the streets.

To make *strattù*, first the homemade passata would be spread over lots of white plates, salted, and left for several days in the hot sun. The warmth of the sun caused the liquid to evaporate. As the days passed, a firmer paste would develop, which had to be repeatedly stirred. Every day, the number of plates would decrease as the increasingly concentrated paste could be spread out on fewer plates (for 100g / 3½oz *strattù* you need about 1kg / 2¼lb tomatoes). You can still buy *strattù* on plates today in little Sicilian stores.

Pasta with tender squash leaves

Pasta con i tenerumi

extra virgin olive oil
2 garlic cloves, ideally pink
garlic, finely chopped
100g (3½oz) pancetta, cut
into little pieces, or
Italian sausagemeat
60g (2oz) tomato purée,
or *strattù* (see p40)
chilli flakes or freshly
ground black pepper
sea salt
handful of basil leaves,
roughly torn
coarse sea salt
200g (7oz) mixture of short
pasta shapes (ruote,
ditalini, zitelli, or small
pieces of broken linguine)
250g (9oz) tender squash or
courgette leaves, torn
15–20 squash or courgette
flowers, torn
50g (1¾oz) young pecorino
cheese, finely chopped,
plus 2 heaped tbsp finely
grated pecorino cheese

The snake gourd (*zucca serpente di Sicilia*) is a quick-growing climbing plant with corkscrew tendrils and beautiful white flowers. The long, narrow squash is harvested from June to September, but its delicate leaves can be consumed as early as May. This pasta dish uses the young, whole, tender leaves (*tenere*). Everything on this wonderful plant is edible: leaves, fruits, and exceptionally delicate flowers, although these wilt quickly. You can use courgette leaves and flowers, too.

Heat 2–3 tbsp olive oil in a sauté pan over a medium heat and lightly sauté the garlic and pancetta. Add the tomato purée or *strattù* and continue frying gently. Pour in 500ml (18fl oz) of boiling water. Season to taste with chilli and salt, scatter in the basil, and simmer everything for 10–15 minutes.

Fill a large saucepan with plenty of water and place over a high heat. When it comes to the boil, sprinkle in coarse sea salt and cook the pasta until *al dente* (usually 1 minute less than the time stated on the packet). During the final minute, carefully stir

in the squash leaves and flowers. Then drain the pasta, retaining some of the water.

Stir the pasta into the sauce along with the leaves, flowers, and chopped cheese. Simmer everything for another minute, then season again with salt and chilli. Depending on the consistency, stir in 100–200ml (3½–7fl oz) of the cooking water. It should be slightly liquid, but not a soup.

Arrange on 2 plates, sprinkle with the grated pecorino and drizzle with a dash of olive oil to serve.

Black pasta with squid

Pasta al nero

400g (14oz) small cuttlefish
  or squid
2 tbsp extra virgin olive oil,
  (I like Nocellara del
  Belice for this), plus
  extra to serve
3 garlic cloves, ideally pink
  garlic, sliced
4 sun-dried tomatoes in oil,
  finely chopped
sea salt
120ml (4fl oz) white wine
coarse sea salt
320g (11oz) squid ink pasta
chilli flakes
handful of flat-leaf
  parsley leaves, chopped
4 tbsp finely grated *ricotta
  salata*, or pecorino cheese

This black pasta dish is common in the province of Syracuse, but it's also often cooked in the Messina and Catania areas, so it's hard to say exactly which region this pasta belongs to now, although Syracuse has plenty of advocates. In Catania, the dish is often modelled on Mount Etna, with some tomato sauce on top for the "fire" and grated *ricotta salata* for the "snow". The black colour of the pasta comes from the squid ink (sepia) which is added to the dough. Because squid ink is rather hard to find, I have used ready-made pasta here, which is fairly easy to buy. The original recipe made with fresh ink does have a more intense flavour, so, if you want to try that, you can get ink sachets at good fishmongers.

Wash the cuttlefish or squid under running water, pulling off the black outer skin as you do this. Dab dry with kitchen paper. Separate the body and tentacles above and below the eyes. Turn the tentacles inside out, press out the innards, and discard. Press out the cuttlebone or cartilage and discard. Reserve 8 cuttlefish or squid, then slice the remaining cuttlefish into rings.

Heat the olive oil in a large pan and sauté the garlic along with the tomatoes. The garlic should not take on any colour. Add the cuttlefish or squid, season with salt, and simmer for 5–7 minutes. Deglaze with the wine and let the alcohol evaporate slightly.

Fill a large saucepan with plenty of water and place over a high heat. When it comes to the boil, sprinkle in coarse sea salt and cook the pasta until *al dente* (usually 1 minute less than the time stated on the packet). Then scoop it out with a slotted spoon and add it – still dripping wet – to the pan with the cuttlefish or squid. Combine well.

Arrange on 4 plates, scatter with chilli flakes, parsley, and *ricotta salata,* and drizzle with a dash of olive oil to serve.

Pasta with ricotta, kumquats, and tuna bottarga

Pasta con ricotta, mandarino cinese, e bottarga di tonno

coarse sea salt
320g (11oz) bucatini or long
thin macaroni
20g (³⁄₄oz) pine nuts
4–6 kumquats
1 tbsp honey
400g (14oz) ricotta
80g (2³⁄₄oz) pecorino cheese,
finely grated
handful of flat-leaf
parsley leaves, chopped
sea salt and freshly ground
black pepper
4 tbsp grated tuna bottarga
(salted roe)
finely grated zest of
1 organic lemon
extra virgin olive oil

Kumquats come originally from south-east Asia. In Cantonese, they are known as "kam kwat" (gold-orange), while in Italy they are called "Chinese mandarins" and are mainly grown in Liguria and Sicily. The fruit is absolutely tiny, as is the tree on which it grows. As a consequence, it is often completely overlooked. Such a small fruit obviously doesn't have much flesh, but the little it does have offers both a sweetness and a certain acidity, and can provide vast quantities of vitamins. In this recipe, I caramelize the flesh of the little citrus to mitigate its often overwhelming acidity. The residual tart flavour then blends beautifully with the salty, rich bottarga.

Fill a large saucepan with plenty of water and place over a high heat. When it comes to the boil, sprinkle in coarse sea salt and cook the pasta until al dente (usually 1 minute less than the time stated on the packet).

Meanwhile, toast the pine nuts in a dry frying pan. Wash the kumquats, trim the ends, and slice the fruit. Bring the honey to the boil with 1 tbsp water in a small pan over a medium heat and cook the kumquat slices in this liquid until caramelized. Remove the pan from the heat.

Drain the pasta, reserving some of the cooking liquid. Return the pasta to its cooking pan while still wet. Mix in the ricotta, pecorino, and some of the pasta water, then fold in the toasted pine nuts, parsley, and caramelized kumquat slices. Season everything to taste with salt and pepper.

Divide the pasta and sauce between 4 plates. Sprinkle with bottarga and lemon zest and drizzle with a dash of olive oil to serve.

Ravioli with radicchio, ricotta, and mortadella

Ravioli con radicchio, ricotta, e mortadella

For the pasta dough
200g (7oz) fine "00" grade
  durum wheat semolina
  flour, plus extra to dust
1 medium egg
sea salt
50ml (1³/₄fl oz) beetroot juice

For the stuffing
110g (4oz) mortadella
  (Italian sausage)
70g (2¹/₄oz) radicchio (red
  parts only)
freshly ground black pepper
40g (1¹/₂oz) pecorino cheese,
  finely grated
200g (7oz) ricotta, plus
  6 tbsp to serve
20g (³/₄oz) dried breadcrumbs,
  or *mollica secca* (see p30)
freshly grated nutmeg

coarse sea salt
4 tbsp butter, softened
4 tbsp finely grated *ricotta
  salata* cheese
2 heaped tbsp pine nuts
extra virgin olive oil
handful of basil leaves

Ravioli is often linked to the food of the north of Italy, particularly Emilia-Romagna. But it is a popular pasta dish in Sicily too, where you can even eat it as a dessert, known as *raviolo dolce di ricotta*, or *cassatella dolce fritta*. Most savoury fillings in Sicily include ricotta, or a combination of cheese and sausagemeat. I've opted for a combination of both these fillings: ricotta and mortadella. And for the first and last time in this cookbook, we are using butter in a savoury dish and egg in the pasta dough.

To make the ravioli dough, knead together the flour and egg with a pinch of salt and the beetroot juice until you have a compact, firm dough. Cover with an inverted bowl and leave to rest at room temperature for at least 30 minutes.

Meanwhile, to make the filling, finely chop together the mortadella and radicchio. Sauté gently in a dry pan to allow some of the liquid to evaporate. Season with pepper and leave to cool slightly, then mix with the pecorino, ricotta, and breadcrumbs, and season with nutmeg. Taste and adjust the seasoning if desired.

Roll out the dough on a floured work surface until it is about 3mm (⅛in) thick and place 1 tbsp piles of the filling mixture at roughly 5cm (2in) intervals on half of the rolled-out pasta. Fold the other half of the pasta dough over the filling and press it down firmly around each little pile, removing as much air as possible in the process. Using a circular ravioli cutter, stamp out the pasta parcels and press the edges down firmly, so any remaining air is removed.

Fill a large saucepan with plenty of water and place over a high heat. When it comes to the boil, sprinkle in coarse sea salt and cook the ravioli for 4–5 minutes. Meanwhile, melt the butter gently in a large saucepan.

Lift the ravioli out of the water with a slotted spoon and toss them carefully in the butter for about 1 minute.

Arrange the ravioli on 6 plates, add 1 tbsp ricotta to each serving, and scatter over the *ricotta salata* and pine nuts. Drizzle with a dash of olive oil and serve sprinkled with basil leaves.

Serves 4
Prep 40 mins

Pasta with Trapani pesto

Busiate con pesto Trapanese

For the pasta dough

400g (14oz) wholegrain
   durum wheat semolina
   flour or 140g (5oz) fine
   durum wheat semolina
   flour and 260g (9¼oz)
   emmer flour, plus extra
   to dust
sea salt

For the pesto

400g (14oz) cherry tomatoes
2 large garlic cloves,
   ideally pink garlic,
   roughly chopped
40g (1¼oz) smoked almonds,
   roasted and salted
50g (1¾oz) basil leaves,
   ideally from basil with
   small intensely flavoured
   leaves, plus extra to serve
2½ tbsp extra virgin olive
   oil (I use Nocellara del
   Belice for this), plus
   extra to serve
freshly ground black pepper

coarse sea salt
4 tbsp finely grated
   or finely chopped
   pecorino cheese

Busa is the name used to refer to the stalk of the diss grass, a variety of Mediterranean grass traditionally used to tie up sheaves of corn. These stalks were also used to roll up fresh pasta in spirals, before they were left to dry. Busiate are a typical pasta of the Trapani province. As with many products that belong to a particular Sicilian region, it is virtually unknown and hard to track down at the other end of the island! For the pesto, I have added unblanched, smoked almonds; in the original, blanched almonds are used.

To make the pasta, combine the flour with a good pinch of salt on a work surface. Gradually knead in 200–250ml (7–9fl oz) of lukewarm water to create a compact, homogeneous dough. Cover and leave to rest at room temperature for 30 minutes.

Meanwhile, remove and discard the stalks from the tomatoes and place in a large bowl. Pour over boiling water from the kettle to just cover and leave for 30 seconds, then drain. The skins should slip off. Discard the skins, roughly chop the flesh, and put in a bowl. Roughly pound the garlic and almonds using a mortar and pestle. Combine two-thirds of this mixture with the tomatoes.

In a mortar and pestle, crush the basil leaves with a pinch of sea salt and the 2½ tbsp olive oil, working it in gradually. Fold the basil paste into the tomato mixture. Season to taste, then leave to infuse for at least 30 minutes.

Roll out the dough on a floured work surface until about 5mm (¼in) thick, then slice into 10–12cm- (4–5in-) long strips. Twist each one around a floured rod, for instance a knitting needle, then pull it off and place on a floured cloth (see overleaf for a photograph of the process).

Fill a large saucepan with plenty of water and place over a high heat. When it comes to the boil, sprinkle in coarse sea salt and cook the pasta until *al dente*.

Drain the pasta and mix well with the pesto, then arrange on 4 plates. Crumble the remaining garlic and almonds over the pasta, drizzle with a dash of olive oil, and serve sprinkled with basil leaves. Offer the pecorino in a bowl on the table.

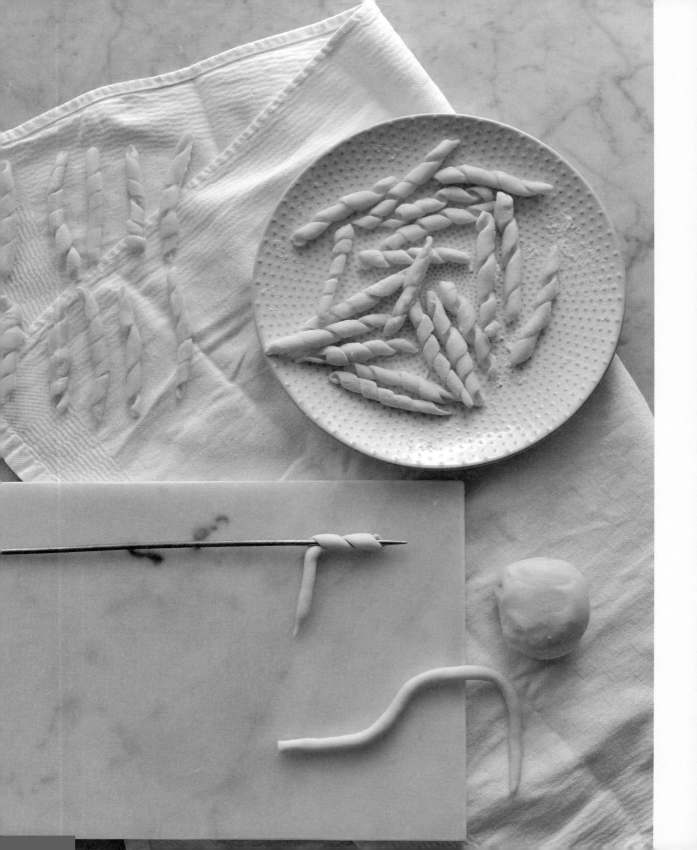

-Couscous-

-Ruote-

-Spaccatelle-

-Anelli-

-Busiate-

-Pasta col nero-

-Cataneselle-

-Mafaldine-

-Sedani-

Secondi

IL MARE

If you want to travel to Sicily, there is no avoiding the sea. And the oceans love Sicily so much that the island is embraced by three seas. To the north there is the Tyrrhenian Sea, to the east lies the Ionian Sea, and to the south the Mediterranean. Perhaps it was these three seas that lovingly moulded Sicily into its triangular shape, giving the island its nickname *Trinacria* ("three-pointed").

Salvatore likes to gesticulate while talking but, because he is driving today, his hands need to stay firmly on the wheel. His sea water production facilities, and his home, are both located in Graniti and, during the drive there, our conversation is about the sea. "The salt content in the Mediterranean is high, at about 38 grams (1½oz) of salt minerals per litre (1¾ pints) of sea water, while the average for the world's oceans is only around 35 grams (1¼oz)."

Why do we need to know this? Because this relatively high level of salt makes a big difference: Mediterranean king prawns taste better than prawns from anywhere else, precisely because their inherent salt content is higher, Salvatore tells me. Together with four other partners in his Aquamaris business, he makes the most of the Mediterranean's salt levels by marketing sea water to the food industry. Top chefs know this ingredient well and have been using it for a long time, but have kept it secret. They know about the special flavour it imparts. Sea water does not just consist of water and sodium chloride (salt), it also contains more than 50 other minerals, and it has been discovered that this specific composition works as a flavour enhancer, making sea water an even more effective form of seasoning than salt itself. By cooking with sea water, you achieve more flavour, getting the most out of fish, tomatoes, and meat. The use of sea water in cooking can also reduce the amount of salt you need to add to any recipe by up to 30 per cent.

As well as the health benefits and flavour potential, Salvatore and his business partners were also motivated by tradition. Salvatore tells me that people are always exclaiming: "'What is it with you and your sea water obsession!' Why? Because even as a child I was always having to fetch sea water for cooking." In Sicily, fresh water is a precious commodity, so why would you add salt to fresh water when you've already got such a large amount of salt water all around? People in coastal areas would always have cooked with sea water in the past,

and fishermen would have prepared fish using sea water, though in those days, no-one understood the mysterious properties of the minerals involved.

Provided sea water is not heated above 100–110°C (212–230°F) it retains a proportion of iodine, which in regular salt is removed during the refinement process, along with all its other minerals. The only alternative to sea water is unrefined salt: not sea salt flakes, but pure salt crystals, the chunks that are left behind during salt production. These are so hard that you can only use them after grating with a sharp blade, and they are also almost impossible to find on sale.

This gave Bruno Patanè, now the managing director at Aquamaris, the idea of reviving the art of cooking with sea water. His original idea was focused entirely on health. Bruno's father Leonardo, a well-known heart surgeon from Catania, was brought on board and, together with a nutritional adviser, they carried out some initial research and analysis. Other business partners

were sought, and that is how Salvatore and his family – the Testas – got involved. As one of Catania's longest established fishing families, they were able to collect large quantities of sea water on their giant ships from depths of 30–40 metres (33–44 yards) and 14 nautical miles off the island's coast. Salvatore was asked to work on product development and Beniamino Sciacca, a chemist, joined the team to work on the purification process. In 2018, the first sea water was sold.

However, before it can be sold, the sea water collected by the fishing boats undergoes a laborious purification process. The preliminary analyses are conducted on board the boats. First the water is tested for heavy metals. If any are found, the water is dumped. (Regardless of the kind of contamination found, if the levels are too high, the water is simply discarded.)

On land, the "harvested water" is conveyed to silos by tankers. Here it is immediately subjected to UV irradiation, which is the first stage in the sterilization process.

Next it is passed through a special resin filter to remove bromine. Even now, the water is not considered to be clean. It still has to pass through various other filters, the smallest of which is just 25 micrometres. Not only does any bacteria or sewage need to be removed, but microplastics are also an issue, and this poses a significant problem. It's even more serious out at sea but, nonetheless, the microplastic causes the filters to become contaminated more quickly and results in a need to change them more frequently.

Once the purification process is complete, the sea water is microbiologically pure and no longer contains any microplastic residues. Right at the end, the sea water undergoes additional sterilization treatment in a UV tunnel. Once it is packed into 1-litre (1¾-pint) bottles or 5-litre (8¾-pint) boxes, it undergoes a final sterilization process. Sea water is a precious commodity that humans would be able to use without processing, and for free, if we had not been so reckless in our conduct towards nature and the environment, actions which are now also having an impact on ourselves.

Professional chefs immediately became the company's first customers. One of these was the outstanding young Sicilian chef Giovanni Santoro, from Linguaglossa. He uses the water for baking bread and also for cooking chicken breasts, which he marinates for 12 hours in sea water before cooking them in a sous-vide machine. The result is a delicacy reminiscent of *prosciutto crudo*. Drinks such as gin or beer can also be made using sea water. (The beer, in particular, goes down very well.)

Salvatore even preserves Datterini tomatoes in sea water; these simply need to be puréed and seasoned with a touch of pepper – perfect. He is also thinking about making a stock with sea water that would contain all those precious minerals. And he has plenty of other ideas, too…

Steamed scabbard fish with tomatoes

Spatola in umido

800g (1³/₄lb) gutted and
  scaled scabbard fish,
  or mackerel
2 garlic cloves, sliced
handful of flat-leaf
  parsley leaves,
  roughly chopped
250g (9oz) plum tomatoes
sea salt and freshly ground
  black pepper
splash of lemon juice
2–3 tbsp extra virgin
  olive oil

The scabbard fish, also known as *pesce sciabola* or *pesce bandiera*, is a type of oily fish, like sardines, anchovies, mackerel, and herring, that has always been affordable for poorer people and so is found in the traditional cuisine of Sicily's less well-off inhabitants. Its delicate white flesh is particularly appreciated in Messina, where it is also referred to as *a signurina du mari* (**"the lady of the sea"**). Scabbard fish is not often found in UK fishmongers, but you can buy it online.

Rinse the fish under running water (don't dry it) and cut it into large fillets. Discard the stalks from the tomatoes and quarter them.

Put the fish in a deep saucepan with the garlic, parsley, tomatoes, some salt and pepper, the splash of lemon juice, and the olive oil. Cover and cook over a medium heat for no more than 10 minutes. And it's ready!

Serves 2
Prep 25 mins, plus extra
   to clean the anchovies

Fried anchovies with mint

Masculini con la menta

20 fresh anchovies, or
   frozen can also be used
about 40g (1¹/₄oz) fine "00"
   grade durum wheat
   semolina flour
extra virgin olive oil
2 garlic cloves, sliced
around 2 handfuls of mint
   leaves, roughly torn, plus
   mint leaves and flowers
   to serve
4 tbsp white wine vinegar
sea salt
chilli flakes

This recipe can also be made using fresh sardines, if you prefer, or if they are easier to find. In Sicily anchovies are called *masculini*, whereas in Italy they are known as *alici* or *acciughe*; the Sicilian name translates literally as "little men". In the Gulf of Catania, which stretches between Capo Mulini and Capo Santa Croce in Augusta, such is the quality of the anchovies that they have a Slow Food designation: *la masculina da magghia*. They are caught by just a few fishing families between April and July only, using an old technique that has a positive impact on the flavour.

Prepare the anchovies in the same way as for the sardines on p64.

Rinse the gutted anchovies and dab dry thoroughly with kitchen paper. Fold the filleted fish closed and turn them in a plate of the flour to coat, then gently shake off any excess.

Heat a generous quantity of olive oil in a sauté pan over a medium–high heat and sauté the anchovies until golden brown. Remove the fish from the pan, reduce the heat, and gently fry the garlic in the same oil, adding more if necessary. Return the fish to the pan and scatter with mint. Pour in the vinegar, immediately cover the pan, and remove from the heat.

Leave the fish to stand for about 1 minute, then season with salt and chilli. Sprinkle the anchovies with a few mint leaves and flowers to serve.

Stuffed sardines on a skewer

Sarde a beccafico alla Palermitana

20 fresh sardines
200g (7oz) fresh
   breadcrumbs, or *mollica
   fresca* (see p30), plus
   2 tbsp extra
4 tbsp flat-leaf
   parsley leaves
2 garlic cloves
2–3 tbsp orange juice
40g (1¼oz) raisins
40g (1¼oz) pecorino cheese,
   finely grated
2 large eggs, lightly beaten
10g (¼oz) pine nuts
1 heaped tbsp pistachios
2 large organic oranges, zest
   removed with a zester
sea salt and freshly ground
   black pepper or chilli
   flakes
extra virgin olive oil
   (I use Tonda Iblea)
16 bay leaves

The original ingredient in this dish was the *beccafico*, a little bird (the garden warbler, to be precise), with a fondness for eating figs. In the 19th century, they would have been served to aristocratic families in Sicily by the Monsù (see p86). This lower budget version uses more affordable and easily obtainable sardines. There are lots of variations on this recipe: in Palermo the fish are usually rolled up and prepared with oranges. In Catania the orange is omitted and the fish are folded together, brushed with a filling, then fried one on top of another like a sandwich.

Remove the scales from the sardines under running water. Hold the fish with the stomach facing up. Bend the head of the sardine gently downwards towards its back and simultaneously make a slit with your thumbnail along the stomach towards the tail fin, to split the stomach. Pinch the lower end of the back bone and pull this out towards the head, pulling off the head with the innards. Rinse the sardines under running water, open them like a book and dab them dry thoroughly with kitchen paper.

Blitz the breadcrumbs with the parsley, garlic, and orange juice in a food processor to create a purée. Mix in the raisins, pecorino, eggs, pine nuts, pistachios, and some of the orange zest. Add salt and season with pepper or chilli flakes, if you prefer. If the consistency is too firm to spread, add some olive oil.

Preheat the oven to 200°C (400°F/ Gas 6) and line a baking tray with baking parchment.

Slice the oranges and cut each round in half. Spread all the sardines with a generous 1 tbsp of the paste. Poke a skewer through a bay leaf. Then fold the tail of one sardine upwards and skewer the sardine too. Next slide an orange slice onto the skewer, followed by the head end of the sardine. Start again with a bay leaf and continue in this way until the first 10 sardines are on the skewer. Prepare the second skewer in exactly the same way.

Lay both skewers on the prepared tray and sprinkle with the 2 tbsp of breadcrumbs. Drizzle with olive oil and bake for around 20 minutes.

Remove, and arrange 5 sardines per person on a plate, drizzling with a dash of olive oil to serve.

Serves 4
Prep 30 mins

Tuna in a pistachio and sesame crust with sweet pickled peppers

Tonno in crosta di pistacchi e sesamo con peperoni all'agrodolce

For the peppers
800g (1³/₄lb) red peppers, ideally Romano peppers
100ml (3¹/₂fl oz) extra virgin olive oil, plus extra for cooking
80g (2³/₄oz) capers in salt
20g (³/₄oz) mint leaves, roughly torn, plus more leaves to serve
15–20g (¹/₂–³/₄oz) honey
4 tbsp lemon juice
chilli flakes
sea salt

For the fish
4 tuna steaks, each 250g (9oz) and roughly 2cm (³/₄in) thick
80g (2³/₄oz) pistachios, plus extra to serve
10g (¹/₄oz) black sesame seeds
30g (1oz) dried breadcrumbs, or *mollica secca* (see p30), finely ground
freshly ground black pepper
extra virgin olive oil

Here tuna is served with preserved peppers, which you might be more familiar with as antipasti, but I've discovered that they also work really well with this pistachio and sesame tuna. Of course, the preserved peppers can also simply be served as a starter. To see a photograph for this recipe, see p177.

Preheat the grill to 200°C (400°F/ Gas 6).

Wash the peppers, prick them all over with a toothpick, coat lightly in oil, and place in a baking dish. Roast in the middle of the grill until the skin begins to blister and turn black in places, turning them every so often.

Remove the tuna from the refrigerator and leave at room temperature until ready to use.

Leave the peppers to cool in a sturdy, food-safe paper bag. Once they are cool enough to handle, pull off and discard the skins and seeds and tear them into strips.

Rinse the capers thoroughly and combine them in a bowl with the pepper strips, mint, honey, lemon juice, the 100ml (3¹/₂fl oz) of olive oil, and a pinch of chilli flakes. Add salt sparingly, as the capers may already be salty enough. Mix well, cover, and leave to infuse for at least 30 minutes.

Crush the pistachios in a mortar and pestle, then mix with the sesame seeds and breadcrumbs in a deep bowl. Season with salt and pepper.

Rub the tuna liberally with olive oil. Turn the fish in the pistachio and sesame mixture to coat, pressing gently to help it stick.

Heat some more olive oil in a frying pan and fry the tuna steaks for 2–3 minutes on each side, until pink.

Arrange the fish with the peppers on 4 plates, sprinkle with mint leaves and pistachios, and serve immediately.

Salt cod with olives, capers, and pears

Stocco alla ghiotta con pere

500g (1lb 2oz) salt cod
freshly ground black pepper
4 tbsp "00" pasta flour
extra virgin olive oil
150g (5¹/₂oz) onions, sliced
    into rings
2 garlic cloves, chopped
1¹/₂ celery sticks, sliced
200ml (7fl oz) white wine
600g (1lb 5oz) passata
40g (1¹/₄oz) tomato purée, or
    strattù (see p40)
60g (2oz) capers in salt
60g (2oz) raisins
80g (2³/₄oz) green olives,
    pitted
2 tsp dried oregano
sea salt
chilli flakes
400g (14oz) waxy potatoes,
    peeled
300g (10oz) pears (about 2),
    unpeeled, finely sliced

This traditional dish with pears is no longer as widespread as it once was. There is incredible variety when it comes to pears on Sicily, including wild pears, some of which are tiny. For this recipe, I recommend a variety such as *pera spinella*, a medium-sized fruit with yellow skin and red patches. The flesh is firm, sweet, and not too juicy, which makes it ideal for cooking. After harvesting in the autumn the pears can be kept until April, while salt cod is mainly served over winter. So this recipe is a fabulous winter meal.

Cut the fish into large chunks and trim off the fins if necessary. Then soak the fish for 2 days in cold water, changing the water several times each day.

After soaking, dab the pieces of fish dry with kitchen paper. Season lightly with pepper, then turn in the flour.

Heat some olive oil in a casserole dish and sauté the pieces of fish briefly on both sides. Remove and set aside.

Sauté the onions, garlic, and celery in the same oil. Deglaze with white wine. Then stir in the passata, tomato purée or *strattù*, and 800–900ml (1¹/₄–1¹/₂ pints) of water and simmer everything briefly. Tip the capers into a sieve and rinse well. Stir them into the tomato sauce along with the raisins, olives, and oregano. Season to taste with salt and chilli flakes.

Slice the potatoes in half lengthways, then cut each half into thirds lengthways. Cook the potatoes in the tomato sauce over a low heat until just tender, adding some boiling water if the sauce becomes too thick.

Add the pears and fish to the sauce. Continue cooking for 8–10 minutes, turning the fish only once in this time and not moving it around too much. Remove from the heat and leave the stew to stand for a few minutes.

Arrange on 4 plates and drizzle with a dash of olive oil to serve.

IL AGRODOLCE

In cooking, opposites are often paired together in order to create a third quality. Neither ingredient should be given more weight than the other; the goal is to achieve balance, because through this interplay something quite new and different is created.

Sicily is an island that is full of opposites in its nature and history. Perhaps that is why a very specific culinary trend has prevailed in Sicily; namely the incorporation of sweet and sour flavours in savoury dishes, a style of cooking known in Italian as *all'agrodolce*.

This approach to combining flavours is known throughout Italy, such as in the renowned Venetian dish of *sarde in saor* (sardines marinated in vinegar). But the trend is even more pronounced in Sicily. No doubt this is partially due to the island's numerous Arabic and Asian influences, and the Arabs do seem to have been the first to use and successfully master the *agrodolce* technique. Another factor in its popularity is surely the Sicilian heat. Acidity and sugar are both excellent preserving agents, and, in the time before refrigeration was available, preserving food was even more important than its flavour. Acids,

such as vinegar, kill off bacteria (which is also why you should wash your chopping boards with vinegar), while sugar — just like salt — draws out water from food, thus inhibiting the formation of mould. A lucky by-product is the deliciousness that the combination creates.

So vinegar and sugar function as excellent substitutes for a refrigerator. Sugar was first introduced to Sicily by the Arabs, but honey and dried fruit can also be used as sweeteners, which is why raisins are so frequently included in Sicilian recipes. Vinegar, usually white wine vinegar, can be substituted by using Sicily's abundant citrus fruits. Oranges, mandarins, clementines, and even kumquats (see p46) — not to mention pomegranates, apples, and in fact most fruits — naturally have a wonderful balance between sweetness and acidity. If this balance in the fruit is not right, the flavour suffers. So nature itself serves as a model for the *agrodolce* approach.

Sicilians just cannot resist this particular style of cooking and the way it encapsulates a natural phenomenon. The contrast between sweetness and acidity also works beautifully with game. One of the most popular meat dishes to showcase this culinary trick is the Sweet-sour Rabbit, *coniglio all'agrodolce* (see p76). In days gone by, meat would have been a rarity for the poorer inhabitants of the island, but a welcome exception to this was most wild game and offal.

Probably the three most popular Sicilian *all'agrodolce* recipes are *Caponata* (see p90), the aforementioned *coniglio all'agrodolce,* and *zucca all'agrodolce* (see p111),

which is the most popular way to eat pumpkin on the island. The list of dishes on Sicily that are prepared *all'agrodolce* is never-ending.

In addition to sugar or honey, and vinegar or citrus juice, there is another typical Sicilian ingredient that is found in virtually all dishes prepared *all'agrodolce*: the caper, ideally from the islands of Pantelleria or Salina.

So I paid a visit to Gaetano Marchetta on Salina, who produces capers there in addition to Malvasia wine. He explained that there are three types of capers sold: very small ones, medium-sized varieties, and very large capers, in which the internal flower is already highly developed. Capers are the unopened flower buds and, naturally, the larger the caper is, the more developed this bud will be (incidentally, the blossom is among the most

beautiful and fragile you will find, see above). Many people are under the impression that the smallest capers are the best quality, but on Salina they don't agree. Here, large capers are the most popular, precisely because you can also taste the flower. You will also find *i cucunci* available. These are caperberries, which only develop if you allow the flower to blossom, then wilt.

Caper bushes grow in the unlikeliest of places, including cracks in walls and in between rocks. This is thanks to the lizards that are extremely fond of the plant and its fruit. The seeds get stuck to the lizards' bodies and they then distribute them all over the island, particularly in sheltered places in stonework, which they love to scurry along.

Sweet-sour rabbit

Coniglio all'agrodolce

extra virgin olive oil
600g (1lb 5oz) waxy potatoes,
  peeled and roughly
  chopped
200g (7oz) onions, roughly
  chopped
50g (1³/₄oz) celery, thickly
  sliced
60g (2oz) capers in salt
800g (1³/₄lb) rabbit, chopped
  into large pieces
70ml (2¹/₂fl oz) white wine
5 sage leaves, plus more
  to serve
2 rosemary sprigs
100g (3¹/₂oz) green olives
50g (1³/₄oz) black olives
35g (1¹/₄oz) raisins
80ml (2³/₄fl oz) white wine
  vinegar
40g (1¹/₄oz) sugar
1 bay leaf
sea salt and freshly ground
  black pepper
mint leaves and flowers,
  to serve

This is one of the most traditional *all'agrodolce*-style meat dishes in Sicily. Nowadays, rabbit is available in supermarkets north of the Alps. Nevertheless, I was astonished when recently I came across a whole rabbit, including its head, at the meat counter in a large German supermarket. In Sicily it's normal to display animals whole, because the philosophy is that you should know what you are eating. People in other countries can find that rather more challenging... If you can't find rabbit where you like, this recipe also works well made with chicken.

Heat a generous slug of olive oil in a casserole dish over a medium heat and sauté the potatoes until they are partially cooked. Set aside.

Heat some more olive oil in the casserole and sauté the onions with the celery. Set aside.

Tip the capers into a sieve and rinse them very well.

Once again, heat some olive oil in the same casserole dish and lightly fry the rabbit on all sides. Deglaze the pan with the wine and allow the alcohol to evaporate briefly. Stir in the onion and celery mixture with the sage, rosemary, olives, raisins, and capers. Pour in sufficient water to just cover, put a lid on, and braise over a medium heat for about 40 minutes, turning the rabbit occasionally during this time.

Add the fried potatoes, plus enough water to just cover them. Combine the vinegar and sugar in a small bowl, pour this in, and add the bay leaf. Season with salt and pepper.

Increase the temperature and continue cooking, uncovered, until the sauce has thickened slightly and the potatoes are tender. You may need to add a little more boiling water, but only ever as much as needed to just about cover the ingredients. Stir occasionally.

Remove and discard the bay leaf. Serve on 4 plates, with sage leaves and mint leaves and flowers.

Serves 2 hungry people
Prep 35 mins, plus 1 day
soaking time

Tripe with black chickpeas

Trippa con ceci neri

120g (4¼oz) black chickpeas
or regular chickpeas
700g (1lb 7oz) prepared
tripe, chopped into
bite-sized pieces
1 heaped tbsp tomato purée,
or *strattù* (see p40)
extra virgin olive oil (I use
Tonda Iblea)
1 red onion, finely chopped
1 carrot, finely chopped
1 celery stick, finely
chopped
450g (1lb) waxy potatoes,
peeled and chopped
2 tbsp roughly chopped
flat-leaf parsley leaves,
plus extra leaves to serve
sea salt and freshly ground
black pepper
chilli flakes

Tripe – unfairly – has a bad reputation. After all, it is low in fat, delicate but with a firm texture, and packed with flavour. In the past, not a single part of a slaughtered animal would have been thrown away, a habit which, sadly, is far from the case now. It's such a shame, as, when combined with foods that are rich in carbohydrates, such as potatoes and pulses, and served with a sharp tomato sauce, tripe has a texture and flavour to surpass any expensive piece of sirloin steak. Try it. You might be converted.

One day in advance, soak the chickpeas in water. When you are ready to cook, drain the chickpeas.

Put the tripe in a saucepan and cover with water. Bring to the boil and cook for 3 minutes. Drain and set aside.

Stir the tomato purée into some water in a small bowl to dissolve.

Heat some olive oil in a pan over a medium heat and sauté the onion, carrot, and celery with the tomato purée mixture. Then stir in the blanched tripe, potatoes, chickpeas, 1 tbsp olive oil, and the parsley. Pour in sufficient water to cover the ingredients by about 1cm (½in). Simmer over a medium heat for about 1 hour, covered partially by the lid. Top up with boiling water occasionally so the ingredients remain covered by 1cm (½in), and stir frequently.

Shortly before the end of the cooking time, season the sauce with salt, pepper, and chilli flakes.

Arrange on 4 plates, drizzle with a dash of olive oil, sprinkle with flat-leaf parsley, and serve immediately.

Serves 4
Prep 1½ hrs, plus
    soaking time

Sweet meatballs with almonds and cinnamon

Polpette dolci

For the sauce
2 tbsp extra virgin olive oil
1 large onion, finely
    chopped
1 large garlic clove, finely
    chopped
1 heaped tbsp tomato purée,
    or *strattù* (see p40)
700g (1½lb) passata
1 cinnamon stick
sea salt and freshly ground
    black pepper

For the meatballs
70g (2¼oz) blanched
    almonds
20g (¾oz) sugar
100g (3½oz) fresh
    breadcrumbs, or *mollica
    fresca* (see p30)
140ml (4½fl oz) milk
480g (1lb 1oz) minced beef
80g (2¾oz) pecorino cheese,
    finely grated
30g (1oz) raisins
20g (¾oz) pine nuts, plus
    extra to serve
1½ tsp ground cinnamon
chilli flakes
2 medium eggs
extra virgin olive oil
oregano leaves, to serve

Polpette are hugely popular in Sicily and made with all kinds of different ingredients, such as aubergines (see p176), ricotta (see p107), or simply with flavoured fresh breadcrumbs. These sweet *polpette* are inspired by a recipe from Maria Grammatico (see p190) in her book *Bitter Almonds*. She describes that, in the post-War years, *polpette dolci* were the favourite festive treat served to children at the San Carlo abbey. The nuns certainly bulked out the meat in their *polpette* with quite a lot of breadcrumbs; Maria halved the quantity in her recipe. The raisins used here would have been those that weren't quite good enough for making dessert.

To make the tomato sauce, heat the olive oil in a pan over a medium heat and fry the onion with the garlic without letting them take on any colour. Stir in the tomato purée or *strattù* along with 400ml (14fl oz) of hot water, bring to the boil, then simmer everything for 1 minute. Stir in the passata and cinnamon stick, season with salt and pepper, and simmer for about 10 minutes.

Meanwhile, to make the meatballs, blitz the almonds and sugar in a food processor until the almonds are reduced to little chunks with just a bit of texture. Soak the breadcrumbs in the milk in a bowl for 20 minutes. Combine the almond mixture and breadcrumbs with the meat, cheese, raisins, pine nuts, and ground cinnamon in a bowl. Season with salt, pepper, and chilli. Now stir in the eggs one at a time. The mixture should not be too firm or too soft.

Heat some olive oil in a frying pan over a medium heat. Use your hands to form 16 meatballs from the mixture. Fry them in the hot oil until golden brown on all sides, then transfer the meatballs to the tomato sauce and simmer gently for another 20 minutes. If the sauce becomes too thick, add some boiling water.

Take 4 deep plates and arrange 4 meatballs and some sauce on each. Scatter each with oregano leaves and pine nuts, grind over some black pepper, and serve drizzled with a dash of olive oil.

Serves 4
Prep 50 mins

Sicilian pork sausages baked with potatoes

Salsiccia al forno con patate

extra virgin olive oil
600g (1lb 5oz) waxy potatoes,
    peeled
1 red onion, finely sliced
sea salt and freshly ground
    black pepper
8 Sicilian sausages with
    fennel, or chunky
    pork sausages
8–10 cherry tomatoes,
    stalks removed, quartered
6 sage leaves, roughly torn
2 rosemary sprigs

Sicilians' favourite way to eat pork is in the form of *salsiccia*, preferably made traditionally using wild fennel seeds and meat from black pigs reared in the Nebrodi mountains. Don't confuse fennel sausages from Tuscany with the Sicilian variety. They are completely different when it comes to appearance, taste, and ingredients. Tuscan *salsiccia al finocchio* is often made using *bardiccio florentino*, a strongly spiced sausage made from beef and pork, which also includes fennel seeds.

Preheat the oven to 200°C (400°F/ Gas 6). Oil a baking tray, or line it with baking parchment.

Cut the potatoes in half lengthways, then slice each half into thirds. Toss the potatoes and onion in a bowl with some salt and pepper and sufficient olive oil to coat everything well. Mix with your hands, then spread the vegetables out on the prepared tray.

Prick the sausages all over with a toothpick and place these on the tray, too. Drizzle the sausages with a small amount of olive oil and slide the tray into the middle of the oven. Toss the vegetables occasionally, and turn the sausages after 15–20 minutes cooking. After about 30 minutes, stir in the tomatoes, sage, and rosemary, season sparingly with salt and continue cooking for about another 10 minutes.

The potatoes and sausages are done when they have turned slightly golden. Remove from the oven and serve.

Piatto unico

IL MONSÙ

In his only novel *The Leopard*, Giuseppe Tomasi di Lampedusa tells the story of an aristocratic Sicilian family during a time of great upheaval on the island. The book begins with the Garibaldi uprising in 1860 and describes the transformation this brought, including the rise of the bourgeoisie. As the plot unfolds, there is frequent mention of the meals taken in noble households at the time. It tells of lavish and flamboyant dishes, served in unusual combinations, conjured up by chefs who toiled night after night over their creations.

These chefs, sweating away in their kitchens, were the superstars of the 18th and 19th centuries during the period of Bourbon rule on the island, which was 1734–1861, and during which Sicily and Naples were temporarily united as a single kingdom ("the Kingdom of the Two Sicilies"). The chefs working in the kitchens of aristocratic houses were referred to as *Monsieur*. At least, that's what people attempted to call them, but Sicilians found the French word almost impossible to pronounce. And that's how it ultimately became *Monsù*. The Neapolitans over on the Italian mainland had similar difficulties, and ended up with their own *Monzù* class.

Cucina dei Monsù was characterized by French influences because, at that time, the French reigned supreme when it came to matters of the kitchen. Acquiring a renowned *Monsù* as their chef came to be a hugely important status symbol for aristocratic families. Sometimes duels were even fought over the services of the most prized cooks. Chefs were elaborately courted and treated with the utmost respect. Anyone who took pride in their culinary skills at the time was obliged to cook French food, but a *Monsù* did not necessarily have to be French.

It is said that the trend was started by Maria Carolina of Austria (Marie Antoinette's sister) when she married King Ferdinand I, ruler of the Kingdom of the Two Sicilies, in 1768. She couldn't stand the simple Neapolitan cuisine, so she asked her sister, who became Queen of France in 1774, to send over French chefs to produce more elegant fare. The less sophisticated Italian chefs she complained about were then trained up to become *Monsieurs* by their French counterparts.

However, this did not result in a sudden replacement of all Sicilian and Neapolitan cooking with French cuisine. Instead, "French" food in the Two Sicilies became simpler and lighter, while the native southern Italian cuisine acquired a more sophisticated tone. It was this mingling of cultures that evolved into *cucina dei Monsù*, a completely new style of cooking, combining the produce of the Two Sicilies with culinary techniques from France. And this food was not confined to aristocratic tables, but found its way to the plates of ordinary people as well. Over many years, *cucina dei Monsù* merged with the simple dishes of *cucina povera* (see p130). In turn, *cucina povera* sought inspiration from *cucina dei Monsù* and tried to imitate this aristocratic cuisine, but with more humble ingredients.

This is why, in Sicily, we find traditional dishes such as *le melanzane a quaglia* ("aubergine in the style of quail"), in which aubergine is used as a substitute for expensive quail. Another island recipe again deploys the aubergine, this time coated in breadcrumbs in the guise of a cutlet.

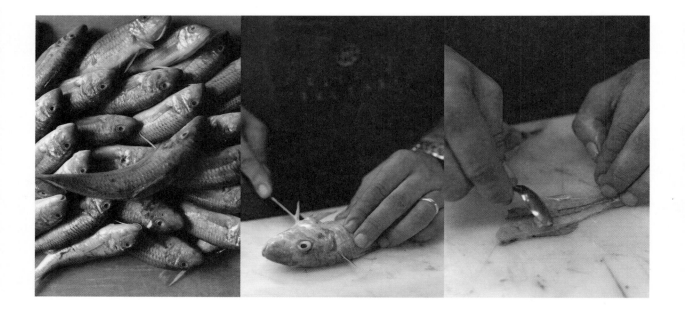

A third example is *sarde a beccafico* (see p64), where sardines are rolled or folded with tails aloft to resemble the pricey little birds on which the nobility would have dined. Or there is the renowned *falsomagro*, a giant rolled roast which, in its *cucina dei Monsù* form, contained peas, ham, provolone, hard-boiled eggs, minced meat... These were replaced among the lower orders by cheaper alternatives; sometimes the meat itself became a frittata. Even moulded savoury *timballi* and cakes, as well as all kinds of *involtini*, originate from *cucina dei Monsù*.

So how did *cucina povera* come to be inspired by aristocratic cooking? Because it was ordinary people, of course, who were in service to the nobility. Domestic staff could see what was going on in the homes of the rich and what kind of food was being served. The exquisite aromas must have been incredibly enticing. No wonder there was a desire to devise versions of these dishes which could be enjoyed at home. And this exchange of influences between the disparate social groups worked in the other direction too. There's no doubt that the servant girls would have chatted with the *Monsù* about their own culinary skills.

Each *Monsù* in turn would have absorbed this knowledge, modifying it somewhat for use in his own creations. After all, a wise *Monsù* understood that his masters were ultimately still Sicilian and always would be. They loved the flavours of their homeland because that was what they had grown up with. No matter how refined French cuisine might be, it could never entirely replace the culinary memories of a Sicilian childhood.

When you look at things from this perspective, you cannot consider Sicilian cooking to be simply the cuisine of the poor. Italian cuisine in general is often pigeonholed as nothing more than the quick assembly of a few high-quality products. But this really isn't the case. Sicily was and still is a veritable melting pot in all regards. Foreign cuisines, such as Greek, Roman, Norman, Arabic, Spanish, and that of many other cultures, have mingled with Sicilian cooking. In addition, recipes favoured by poor farmers and fishermen influenced the dining habits of the wealthy aristocrats. Ultimately, three significant styles can be distinguished in Sicilian cuisine: *cibo di strada* (see p112), *cucina povera* (see p130), and *cucina dei Monsù*.

Italian cooking, especially the cuisine of southern Italy, has developed into one of the most loved and imitated styles of food cooked and eaten around the world. French cuisine, on the other hand, has gradually diminished in significance and stature over time – at least when it comes to everyday cooking. Today's Sicilian chefs are well aware of this and hope to avoid the same pitfalls. If you rest on your laurels and resist innovation, they think, sooner or later you will suffer the same fate as the French.

But this is unlikely to happen any time soon. The evolution of Sicilian cuisine has been promoted for several years by an exciting group of new chefs, who have internalized lessons learned from the *Monsù*: they are especially aware that the traditional cooking of the island should neither be devalued nor forgotten. There are numerous products of exceptional quality on the island crying out for new interpretations, while inspiration can often be found by examining the past too.

The island's latest culinary stars include, amongst others: Ciccio Sultano, Patrizia di Benedetto, Martina Caruso, Vincenzo Candiano, Accursio Craparo, Pino Cuttaia, Massimo Mantarro, Natale Briguglio, Alberto Rizzo, Pietro D'Agostino, Vladimiro Farina, Domenico Colonnetta, Francesco Patti, Francesco Mineo, Alfio Visalli, and Giovanni Santoro.

The photographs on this page and on the previous pages depict dishes served by Ciccio Sultano at his two-Michelin-starred Duomo restaurant in Ragusa.

p87, clockwise from top left: Sultano with a filleted red mullet; red mullet tails as part of a finished dish; the finished dish itself, Red mullet with garum and wild barbecued leeks (*Triglia maggiore di scoglio con salsa garum e porri selvatici al BBQ*).
p88: Sultano filleting red mullet.
p89: mis-en-place for the finished dish; the finished dish itself, Spaghettone with North African sauce, tuna bottarga, and carrot juice (*Spagghettone in salsa moresca "Taratatà" con bottarga di tonno e succo di carote*).

Serves 4
Prep 1 hr 20 mins; start the
    previous day or a few
    hours in advance

Caponata with eggs and St Bernardo sauce

Caponata con uova sode e sarsa di San Birnardu

1 portion St Bernardo sauce
    (see p93)
extra virgin olive oil
2 aubergines, chopped into
    4–5cm (2in) pieces
1 large red pepper, cut into
    in 4–5cm (2in) pieces
1 large onion, finely
    chopped
2 tbsp small capers
handful of green olives,
    pitted
1 red chilli, chopped
1 celery stick, chopped
400g (14oz) ripe tomatoes
1 tbsp chopped basil leaves
sea salt
25–30g (1oz) sugar
125ml (4fl oz) white wine
    vinegar
8 medium eggs, hard-boiled
    and shelled

The most famous of all dishes in Sicilian cuisine! In 1869, the Pensabene family began to produce *caponata* on an industrial scale. Sales were particularly successful in America, on account of the number of Sicilian immigrants there. Contrary to common belief, the aubergine doesn't have to go it alone in this dish, there are plenty of other wonderful combinations. The aristocratic version would have been served with fish, but nowadays the more frugal vegetarian version is the most widely found. I serve this *caponata* following an ancient – and now uncommon – recipe using St Bernardo sauce and eggs.

Prepare the St Bernardo sauce (see p93).

Heat some olive oil in a pan over a high heat. Sauté the aubergines first until partially cooked, then set aside. Add more oil if needed and sauté the pepper until partially cooked in the same way, then set aside.

Heat some olive oil in a large saucepan and sauté the onion with the capers, olives, chilli, and celery.

Meanwhile, remove and discard the stalks from the tomatoes and place in a large bowl. Pour over boiling water from the kettle to just cover and leave for 30 seconds, then drain. The skins should slip off. Remove the skins and chop the flesh finely. Add them to the pan with the onion mixture and let them simmer down slightly.

Add the partially cooked aubergine and pepper pieces with the basil, season with salt, and simmer until the vegetables are cooked. Combine the sugar and vinegar in a small bowl, stir this in, and let everything continue to simmer for another 5 minutes. Remove from the heat and leave to cool until lukewarm.

Divide between 4 plates, add a couple of hard-boiled eggs to each and serve with the St Bernardo sauce.

Caponata: the flavours will be even better if the dish is prepared a day in advance. Just reheat it slightly and serve lukewarm, or even at room temperature, but not cold from the refrigerator, which will numb all the flavours.

Serves 4
Prep 30 mins

St Bernardo sauce

Sarsa di San Birnardu

120g (4¼) blanched almonds
50g (1¾oz) dried
breadcrumbs, or
mollica secca (see p30)
6 anchovies in oil
50g (1¾oz) caster sugar, or
honey, plus extra to taste
3 tbsp extra virgin olive
oil, plus extra to taste
(I use Tonda Iblea)
80ml (2¾oz) freshly
squeezed orange juice, plus
extra to taste
60ml (2oz) cider vinegar,
plus extra to taste
70g (2¼oz) dark chocolate

This is an unusual sauce dating back to ancient times, and confirms the Sicilian passion for powerful contrasts. It is thought that it was invented by Benedictine monks from Catania. It is delicious, and embodies a flavour we now know as umami. But today the sauce is far less common on the island. During the *Monsù* period (see p86) it would have been served alongside *caponata*, albeit a more lavish version of the dish than my own recipe (see p90). The sauce also goes well with artichokes, eggs, and meat.

Lightly toast the almonds in a dry pan, leave until cool enough to handle, then chop quite finely.

Meanwhile, lightly toast the breadcrumbs in a dry pan and mix these with the almonds in a bowl.

Finely chop the anchovies and combine with the sugar. Mix this with the olive oil and orange juice, then stir it into the almond mixture. Gradually stir in the vinegar.

Melt the chocolate over a bain-marie (in a heatproof bowl over a saucepan of simmering water, making sure the bowl does not touch the water), then stir this into the sauce. For my tastes the sauce is now ready. However, if desired, you can adjust the flavour with additional sugar, oil, orange juice, and vinegar. The sauce should have a consistency similar to pesto.

Store in the refrigerator for about 1 hour before serving, to allow the flavours to develop. Then serve lukewarm with vegetables or meat.

If covered with cling film, the sauce will keep in the refrigerator for about 3 days. Ideally warm it gently over a bain-marie (see left) before serving.

Serves 6–8
Prep 1¾ hrs, plus
   cooling time

Meat and vegetable pie with pasta and custard filling

Timballo del gattopardo

For the filling
20g (¾oz) dried porcini
100g (3½oz) peas
coarse sea salt
80g (2¾oz) rigatoni
120g (4¼oz) cooked turkey
   ham, finely chopped
1 medium egg
25g (1oz) fresh breadcrumbs
1½ handfuls of flat-leaf
   parsley leaves, chopped
30g (1oz) pecorino cheese,
   finely grated
sea salt and black pepper
extra virgin olive oil
1 shallot, finely chopped
200g (7oz) mixed minced meat
50ml (1¾fl oz) Marsala
4 quail's eggs, hard-boiled
   and shelled
1 black truffle

For the shortcrust pastry
350g (12oz) fine "00" grade
   durum wheat semolina
   flour
pinch of salt
175g (6oz) chilled unsalted
   butter, chopped
1 medium egg
80g (2¾oz) caster sugar
½ tsp ground cinnamon

For the custard
500ml (16fl oz) whole milk
40g (1½oz) cornflour
2 medium egg yolks, plus
   1 medium egg
seeds from 1 vanilla pod
50g (1¾oz) sugar
½ tsp ground cinnamon

Soak the porcini in hot water for 30 minutes, then squeeze out the liquid.

To make the pastry, combine the flour and salt and rub in the butter. Beat the egg with the sugar and cinnamon and work everything together until smooth. Wrap in cling film and place in the refrigerator for 1 hour.

For the custard, mix 100ml (3½fl oz) of the milk with the cornflour, egg yolks, and egg. Use a balloon whisk to mix the vanilla seeds, sugar, and cinnamon into the remaining milk, then heat this in a saucepan. Remove from the hob and pour into the egg mixture in a thin stream, beating constantly. Then return to the pan and place over a medium heat, stirring, until it thickens. Place cling film directly on the surface of the custard and leave to cool. (But don't chill.)

Preheat the oven to 180°C (350°F/ Gas 4). Set aside one-third of the pastry. Roll out the remainder on a floured work surface to 5mm (¼in) thick. Use this to line the base and sides of a 20cm (8in) springform cake tin (9cm/3½in deep). Cover the tin with baking parchment, fill it with baking beans and bake for 12 minutes. Remove the beans and paper and set the pastry shell aside.

Blanch the peas in boiling, salted water for about 5 minutes, immerse them in iced water, then drain. Cook the pasta in boiling, salted water until *al dente*, then drain. Mix the turkey ham, egg, breadcrumbs, ½ handful of the parsley, and the pecorino until you have a firm mixture that can be moulded. Season. Shape into walnut-sized balls, toss in flour and sauté in plenty of olive oil for 3 minutes.

Heat some olive oil in another pan and sauté the shallot. Add the minced meat and continue frying. Deglaze the pan with Marsala and continue simmering for 1–2 minutes. Stir in the peas and porcini, and simmer for another 1–2 minutes. Season to taste and remove from the heat.

Set the oven to 190°C (375°F/Gas 5).

To make the layers: spread half the custard over the pastry base. Scatter over the pasta and cover everything with the minced meat sauce. Arrange the meatballs and quail's eggs on top and grate over the truffle. Season with a touch of pepper. Cover everything with the remaining custard. Roll out a 5mm (¼in) thick lid from the remaining pastry and, if you like, create decorations from any leftovers.

Bake in the centre of the oven for 30–35 minutes, then reduce the temperature to the oven's lowest setting and continue to bake for another 5 minutes until done.

Anchovy and potato tart

Timballo di alici e patate

800g (1³/₄lb) fresh anchovies
400g (14oz) waxy potatoes,
　peeled and cut into 3mm-
　(¹/₈in-) thick slices
coarse sea salt
60g (2oz) dried breadcrumbs,
　or *mollica secca* (see p30)
30g (1oz) almonds, roughly
　chopped
1 large garlic clove, ideally
　pink garlic, finely
　chopped
15g (¹/₂oz) flat-leaf parsley
　leaves, chopped, plus
　extra sprigs to serve
200g (7oz) cherry tomatoes,
　finely chopped
50g (1³/₄oz) pecorino cheese,
　roughly chopped
1 tbsp candied lemon peel
finely grated zest of
　1 organic lemon, plus
　lemon wedge, to serve
1 tsp fennel seeds
sea salt and freshly ground
　black pepper
extra virgin olive oil
　(I like Biancolilla here)

This *timballo* looks intricate and impressive, but the only thing that takes a bit of time is filleting and cleaning the little anchovies. You can also make this recipe with sardines, which of course are slightly larger, so there will be fewer to fillet.

Prepare the anchovies as described for sardines (see p64).

Blanch the potatoes for about 5 minutes in salted, boiling water. Then immerse in cold water.

Put the breadcrumbs, almonds, garlic, parsley, tomatoes, pecorino, candied lemon peel, lemon zest, and fennel seeds into a bowl and mix well. Season the mixture to taste.

Preheat the oven to 200°C (400°F/ Gas 6).

Oil a round baking dish 25cm (10in) in diameter and line it with baking parchment. Arrange half the anchovies on the base with their heads facing towards the centre. Make sure they are neat, as they will be on top once the *timballo* is turned out of the tin. Spread half the potato slices on top, season sparingly with salt and pepper, then scatter over half the breadcrumb mixture. Repeat these layers once more, finishing with the remaining breadcrumb mixture. Season generously with pepper and drizzle liberally with oil.

Bake for 25 minutes in the oven on a low shelf. Move the tin to the centre shelf and continue baking for another 10 minutes.

Let the *timballo* cool down slightly before turning it out of the tin. Serve with a lemon wedge and parsley.

CICCIO

The Sicels founded the settlement of Hybla that today is known as Ragusa Ibla. It forms part of the city of Ragusa, rebuilt in the Sicilian Baroque style following an earthquake in 1693. For a long period this was just an attractive, historic, Baroque old town. Then, in 2002, it was one of the late-Baroque towns of Val di Noto to be declared a UNESCO world heritage site. Two years earlier, in 2000, one of the first restaurants had opened up in the town's Palazzo la Rocca, which in 1961 served as a set for the film *Divorce Italian Style*, directed by Pietro Germi and starring Marcello Mastroianni.

The restaurant is called Duomo, and it currently holds two Michelin stars. It's in a beautiful location, with the Cathedral of San Giorgio just a stone's throw away.

Ciccio Sultano was born "by chance" in Turin in 1970, because his parents happened to be in Piedmont looking for work. It was not long, however, before they returned to Sicily. When Ciccio was four years old, his father died. At the age of 11 he began to work while simultaneously attending school, and managed to keep this up until the age of 13, when, unsurprisingly, something had to give. He broke off his studies in order to work full time. He ended up with a job in a *pasticceria* with a bar and snack counter (*tavola calda*) in Vittoria. Here he learned how to make *dolci* while peering over at the bar to keep an eye on how they put together American cocktails. He left home when he was 17, returned to school, and decided – at the age of 19 – to pursue a career as a chef. At the same time he bought a house. In order to pay for it, he had to put in double shifts. So during the day he worked at the *pasticceria*, and in the evening he worked at a *spaghetteria*.

There was no time for sleep. His passion for cooking was becoming increasingly clear. He began teaching himself, reading books by the great chefs Gualtiero Marchesi, Gianfranco Vissani, Michel Troisgros, and Alain Ducasse. He collected issues of the magazine *Grand Gourmet*. And at the age of 29 he opened his own restaurant, Duomo. In 2004 he was awarded his first Michelin star, and in 2006 he received a second star. The logo of the restaurant incorporates a stylized depiction of what Ciccio believes are the three most important ingredients on the island, the three things essential to being a Sicilian and a chef: olive oil, salt, and wheat (*olio, sale, grano*). In his logo, these three components are artistically combined to create our globe.

Ciccio has never regarded Michelin stars as his overriding motivation; he has simply always wanted to do everything as well as possible. This aspiration comes in part from his upbringing, influenced by his grandparents, but it is also a fundamental characteristic of his very nature. "For me it was just logical, natural, and honest to do everything as well as possible. That's always been my approach, even when I was young. I have always tried to give my maximum effort. That's how today's results have come about," Ciccio tells me.

In 2015, he launched the "multi-concept" bar I Banchi, managed by his former colleague Peppe Cannistrà. You can hang out here in a relaxed atmosphere from breakfast to apéritifs right through to dinner, or you can shop for high-quality products sold under the Ciccio Sultano name. This renowned chef is certainly a great networker, who collaborates with other people in Sicilian food who are keen to make an impact on the world with their great products and high environmental and husbandry standards. This includes Raul and Jessica,

who cultivate an incredible variety of vegetables, plants, and flowers at the Villa Melina in Pedalino, and also possess detailed knowledge about ancient aspects of Sicilian horticulture that was very nearly lost. Ciccio also supports a project called L'Aia Gaia, run by Carmelo Cilia, an absolute expert in Sicilian cheese. He has even helped to create a paradise for chickens, in collaboration with Paolo Moltisanti. The birds do exactly as they please in a free-range environment. He also works with Nino Testa, who belongs to one of the longest established fishing families from Catania (see p56), offering advice on design issues. That's one of Ciccio Sultano's other talents: he possesses a fine eye for the visual arts.

Ten years ago he met Gabriella Cicero. She is multitalented, acting as the general manager and second-in-command for Ciccio's little empire. What he has achieved with his team over a period of nearly two decades has reshaped the entire gastronomic landscape of this island.

"Our cuisine is a bit like that of the Phoenicians," says Ciccio, explaining his food philosophy. "They came here, not as conquerors, but as traders; they would buy something at one port, then sail to the next port and sell it on there. Our cuisine is the expression of many great cultures, that have met, traded, fought, and eaten on this island for more than 4,000 years. So Sicilian food is not just *caponata*, *cannolo*, and *cassata Siciliana* – there's so much more too."

He gives an illustration: "Let's take *biancomangiare*, for example. People were already crazy about it back in Norman times, and this dish was constantly relocating: from Persia to France to Sicily. *Biancomangiare* could be any number of different things. Sometimes it was a sweet dish with almond milk; or with almond and goat milk and added chicken it could be transformed into a thick stew; on other occasions it was served as an antipasto, sometimes as a mousse, or even as a soup." Ciccio continues: "The one thing I want to make clear is that tradition can tempt you into standing still in order to

preserve authenticity, but human evolution depends on everything around it and that includes food. Just as people develop over time, so there are changes in their conduct, their cuisine, and their beliefs. In one sense, culinary evolution can involve a 'betrayal' of tradition. Being 'disloyal' so that something new can be created, making innovation possible. That is what we are doing at Duomo."

Sicily's wonderfully diverse food culture is worth celebrating outside Italy too. In 2018, Ciccio Sultano opened the Pastamara – Bar con Cucina at The Ritz-Carlton in Vienna.

Stuffed baked artichokes with St Bernardo sauce

Carciofi ripieni al forno con sarsa di San Birnardu

For the artichokes
8 artichokes
1 organic lemon
150ml (5fl oz) white wine
1 portion St Bernardo Sauce
  (see p93)

For the stuffing
4 heaped tbsp coarse dried
  breadcrumbs, or *mollica
  secca* (see p30)
2 garlic cloves
6 anchovy fillets in oil
2 heaped tbsp finely chopped
  mint leaves
2 heaped tbsp finely chopped
  flat-leaf parsley leaves
1 tbsp finely grated zest of
  1 organic lemon
extra virgin olive oil
2 heaped tbsp finely grated
  pecorino cheese
sea salt flakes
chilli flakes

To be honest, you could spend a whole day eating artichokes with St Bernardo sauce, so it's always worth making extra while you are at it! A large serving platter is ideal for this dish. Put it in the centre of the table, filled with the stuffed artichokes, along with a couple of little bowls of St Bernardo sauce and some hard-boiled eggs in another bowl alongside. If you like, you can serve this with *caponata* (see p90), plus some fine wine (both red or white work splendidly here). Invite your friends over and time will fly by.

Prepare the artichokes (see p35), then slice them in half lengthways and put them in a bowl of lemon water until ready to use.

Toast the breadcrumbs in a dry pan.

Finely chop the garlic together with the anchovies. Stir the mixture in a bowl with the herbs, lemon zest, toasted crumbs, 4 tbsp olive oil, and the pecorino until well combined. Season with salt and chilli flakes.

Preheat the oven to 160°C (325°F/ Gas 4).

Fill half the artichokes with the stuffing mixture. Place all the artichokes, cut surfaces up, in a casserole or baking dish. Pour over the wine and add 250–300ml (9–10fl oz) of water and drizzle with plenty of olive oil. Cover with foil, pressing it down firmly around the edges of the dish to seal.

Bake the artichoke halves in the centre of the oven for 30–40 minutes. The outer leaves should come away easily at the end of this time. If not, cook for a little longer until they do.

Remove the cooked artichokes, place all the artichoke halves on a serving dish, and sprinkle with sea salt. Serve the unstuffed artichokes with the St Bernardo sauce.

Serves 4
Prep 1 hr 20 mins

Ricotta dumplings in an orange and tomato sauce

Polpette di ricotta col sugo al profumo d'arancia

For the dumplings
80g (2³/₄oz) fresh
   breadcrumbs, or *mollica fresca* (see p30)
200g (7oz) ricotta,
   well drained
25g (scant 1oz) Parmesan
   cheese, finely grated
1 medium egg
1 tbsp finely chopped
   flat-leaf parsley leaves
pinch of zest from 1 organic
   orange, plus extra to serve
freshly grated nutmeg
sea salt and freshly ground
   black pepper

For the sauce
extra virgin olive oil
   (such as Tonda Iblea)
1 large garlic clove,
   finely chopped
1 heaped tbsp tomato purée,
   or *strattù* (see p40)
2 x 400g cans of chopped
   tomatoes
pared zest of ¹/₂ organic
   orange, removed with a
   vegetable peeler, without
   the white pith
small handful of basil
   leaves, plus more to serve
40g (1¹/₂oz) raisins

Orange and tomato is one of my favourite combinations. I have to rein myself in from automatically reaching for an orange every time a recipe involves tomatoes. In the period between October and May, there are oranges in Sicily that range in colour from bright yellow to blood red. In addition to the *Arancia rossa di Sicilia* blood oranges, there are the pale "vanilla oranges" *Arancia di Ribera* and the almost-lost *Arancia ovale della Valle dell'Anapo*, which you will sometimes find as late as June; all of them hold protected origin status. And that's not to mention navel oranges. Even outside the season you find oranges in our gardens, some of which are edible.

To make the dumplings, mix the breadcrumbs, ricotta, Parmesan, egg, parsley, orange zest, and some nutmeg. Season to taste with salt and pepper. Let the ricotta mixture rest in the refrigerator for 15 minutes.

Meanwhile, to make the sauce, heat 2 tbsp olive oil in a saucepan and gently sauté the garlic. Stir the tomato purée or *strattù* in a small bowl with 200ml (7fl oz) of warm water, then pour this into the garlic pan and continue simmering for 1 minute.

Next combine the tomatoes in a mixing bowl with 200ml (7fl oz) of warm water, the pared orange zest, basil, and raisins and add to the pan. Season, then simmer for 20 minutes. Remove and discard the pared orange zest and set aside to keep warm.

Meanwhile, bring a large saucepan of salted water to the boil. Use your hands to shape 12 dumplings from the ricotta mixture and slide these into the boiling water. They need to have plenty of space, so, if necessary, cook them in batches. Once the dumplings have floated to the surface, cook for 8–10 minutes, then scoop them out of the water with a slotted spoon and transfer to the tomato sauce. Leave to stand for about 1 minute.

Arrange the ricotta dumplings with the orange and tomato sauce on 4 plates, scatter with basil leaves and orange zest, and drizzle everything with a dash of olive oil to serve.

Angel hair pasta fritters with pecorino, spinach, date syrup, and cinnamon

Capelli d'angelo con pecorino, spinaci, sciroppo di datteri, e cannella

1kg (2lb 4oz) fresh spinach
coarse sea salt
200g (7oz) angel hair pasta
80g (2³/₄oz) raisins
80g (2³/₄oz) pecorino cheese, finely grated
2 medium eggs, lightly beaten
sea salt and freshly ground black pepper
extra virgin olive oil
date syrup, or honey
ground cinnamon

At first glance, this seems a bewildering combination. Hearty pasta with spinach and sheep's cheese... and a sweet component... plus cinnamon? But this is another ancient and authentic Sicilian recipe. Nowadays, alas, it is a little-known dish. In its original form it would have been sweetened with honey and, curiously, it would traditionally have been made without any egg. Although how on earth the whole thing held together without egg is a complete mystery to me...

Wash the spinach. Get a bowl filled with iced water ready. Put a large saucepan with plenty of water over a high heat. When it comes to the boil, sprinkle in coarse sea salt, and blanch the spinach for 1–2 minutes. Remove with tongs or a slotted spoon, leaving the water in the pan, and immerse in your iced water. Drain, squeeze out any liquid, and put in a bowl.

Return the water to the boil (ensuring you have at least 2 litres/3½ pints) and cook the angel hair pasta until *al dente* (usually 1 minute less than the time stated on the packet). Drain and mix into the spinach in the bowl. Leave to cool slightly.

Meanwhile, cover the raisins with boiling water in a small bowl, leave to stand briefly, then drain and squeeze the raisins well. Combine the raisins with the pasta and spinach, then add the pecorino and eggs. Season to taste with salt and pepper.

Heat some olive oil in a pan and cook portions of pasta "nests" (twisting each with a fork before lifting it into the pan). Fry the "nests" on both sides until crisp.

Arrange these pasta fritters on plates, drizzle with date syrup, and sprinkle with cinnamon to serve.

Mafaldine with lamb and minted sweet-sour squash

Mafaldine con agnello e zucca all'agrodolce alla menta

For the lamb and pasta
320g (11oz) lamb, from the
   leg or neck
extra virgin olive oil
70ml (2¹⁄₂fl oz) medium dry
   red wine
25g (scant 1oz) tomato purée
240g (8oz) canned chopped
   tomatoes
200g (7oz) potatoes, chopped
   into 1 cm (¹⁄₂in) cubes
1 shallot, chopped
2 garlic cloves, chopped
1 carrot, chopped
1 celery stick, chopped
3 parsley sprigs, chopped
sea salt and freshly ground
   black pepper
coarse sea salt
320g (11oz) mafaldine, or
   tagliatelle
4 heaped tbsp finely grated
   pecorino cheese

For the squash
600g (11b 5oz) squash
extra virgin olive oil
80g (2³⁄₄oz) black olives
   (about 20)
2 garlic cloves, sliced
handful of mint leaves,
   roughly chopped, plus
   extra to serve
chilli flakes
2 tbsp white wine or cider
   vinegar
10g (¹⁄₄oz) caster sugar

Usually, sweet-sour squash (*zucca all'agrodolce*) is eaten as a starter, side dish, *piatto unico*, or *intermezzo*. But this combination with lamb and pasta just floated into my head one day. The result is a really attractive, well-balanced dish. The mint in the squash also complements the lamb fabulously.

Remove the lamb from the refrigerator 1 hour before cooking and let it come to room temperature, then chop into 1.5–2cm (¾in) chunks.

Heat some oil in a large saucepan and sear the meat on all sides, then deglaze the pan with the red wine, allowing the alcohol to evaporate slightly. Stir the tomato purée into 200ml (7fl oz) of water in a small bowl and add this to the meat with the chopped tomatoes. Stir, then add the potatoes, the remaining vegetables, and parsley. Season with salt and pepper, cover, and simmer gently until the potatoes are cooked. Stir occasionally during this process and leave the lid off for the final 5 minutes. Adjust the seasoning once done.

For the squash, preheat the oven to 180°C (350°F/Gas 4) and line a deep baking tray with baking parchment. Peel and deseed the squash and chop into 5mm- (¼in-) thick slices. Coat with olive oil in a bowl and season with salt. Arrange on the baking tray.

Press the olives with the flat side of a kitchen knife to help you remove the stones. Scatter the olives over the squash and bake for 10 minutes in the centre of the oven. Then sprinkle over the garlic, mint, and a pinch of chilli flakes. Continue cooking for another 5 minutes. Stir the vinegar and sugar in a small bowl, pour over the squash, and return the tray to the oven for another 5 minutes.

Fill a large saucepan with plenty of water and place over a high heat. When it comes to the boil, sprinkle in coarse sea salt and cook the pasta until *al dente* (usually 1 minute less than the time stated on the packet). Drain and mix with the sauce while still dripping wet.

Make nests of mafaldine and lamb on 4 plates. Arrange the sliced squash on top. Sprinkle with pecorino and mint leaves to serve.

LA STRADA

Il cibo di strada is street food from the Sicilian capital, Palermo. It originally came about as food for the poor, but is different from the traditional cuisine that was cooked at home by women for their families. It was made only to be sold. Palermo's street food is distinctly *Palermitano* and it exists in this form exclusively in Palermo. It is not a wider Italian tradition.

I met up with Giorgio Flaccavento out on the street in front of the entrance to the Teatro Massimo di Palermo. Before Giorgio became a street food guide in Palermo, he worked in marketing in the publishing industry for 14 years, specializing in art and Sicilian tourism. In this role he travelled the length and breadth of Sicily, and, while on the road, he developed a passion for local food specialities and products, and he found that there was always something new to discover.

After his career in publishing he decided he wanted to work in tourism, so he applied for a guide licence and got in touch with the founders of Palermo Street Food.

Palermo Street Food was created by a young couple: Salvatore and Danielle. He is 100 per cent born-and-bred in Palermo, while she is American through and through. As a foreigner, Danielle had a definite instinct for what was unusual about Palermo's food culture and an appreciation for those snacks that local residents take for granted. She knew how to identify exactly which aspects of the city's cuisine deserved more attention. "It's crazy that you have this street food culture that is completely ignored by the tourist industry," she says. And that's how Palermo's first street food tour came into being.

Locals in search of *il cibo di strada* usually head to one of the three largest markets in Palermo old town: the Mercato Ballarò, Mercato della Vucciria, and Mercato del Capo. Nothing unusual is offered there, just simple, everyday food. This food has always existed in Palermo, long before "street food" was even a concept and well before it became so trendy. The only extraordinary thing for the food stall operators is the sudden attention they are now getting! But the recognition is great for business, because in the past there were very few people who appreciated the value and the magic of these markets. One of those select few was the painter Renato Guttuso, who created his famous picture of a bustling market scene, *Vucciria di Palermo*, in 1974.

Many dishes contain offal, such as *la stigghiola* (lamb or kid goat intestine with onion and parsley, roasted on a spit) made by *stigghiularu*; *pani ca meusa* (bread with spleen and lung) made by *meusaru*; *budelle di vitello* (calf intestine); *musso e carcagnolo* (using meat from the cheek and heel); *lingua* (tongue); *mammelle della mucca* (cow's udder); and even *pene del vitello* (calf's penis).

All these dishes use innards and offal that are eaten here (and only here) in Palermo. Another speciality from Palermo is the slightly less alarming *panelle e crocchè* (chickpea slices and croquettes), a dish without any offal, which tourists (unsurprisingly) usually prefer!

Of course, this recipe has now been copied elsewhere in Sicily and you may find it offered as an *aperitivo*, but you will only find it served as street food in Palermo. Some books incorrectly claim that *panelle e crocchè* is the quintessential Sicilian street food. But before all the street food hype, you would barely have encountered anyone in Catania who had eaten or heard of this dish. The same is true of the following recipes: *la rascatura*, which is made using the leftover dough from *panelle e cazzilli*, "cobbling" the bits together to make something new, because nothing should be wasted or thrown away; *lo sfincione* (focaccia Palermo style); *la frittola* (veal scraps that are cooked, then browned in lard) made by the *frittularu*; *la quarume* (made from various bits of beef tripe); *il polpo* (octopus)

served as street food and – of course – stuffed rice balls, which are well known in Catania, but which take the feminine linguistic form here (*arancine*) and are round rather than cone-shaped (see p122).

As well as being the capital of Sicily, Palermo is also the capital of outdoor gastronomy. The city's street food culture is incredibly diverse and its traditions go back a long way. Many recipes have a history spanning centuries, as well as origins far beyond the capital city itself. For instance, the traditional dish *pani ca meusa* (bread with spleen and lung) is thought to go back to medieval times, when the Jews in Palermo worked as butchers, following Hebrew rituals. Their religion prohibited them from accepting money for meat that had been slaughtered in the Kosher tradition. However, the same did not apply to offal, so this was turned into a dish to be sold to their customers. Following the expulsion of the Jews in the 15th century, the recipe was initially forgotten, but it has been resurrected by the residents of Palermo.

Another factor in the widespread consumption of offal was the level of meat consumption by the island's numerous aristocratic families. Even in the ancient days, slaughterhouse waste would have been discarded, so the poor took advantage of this out of sheer necessity.

Many visitors who book a street food tour with Giorgio are surprised at how varied the food in Palermo is. It exceeds their expectations. But it is easier to understand this variety if you remember that Sicily is the product of numerous different rulers. What we see in the island's food today is its multicultural inheritance from more than 10 different countries of provenance.

Sicily is a veritable melting pot, and not just in the kitchen. Each of its prevailing regimes has also left its own architectural traces. As a consequence, Giorgio tells me, food and architecture have a lot in common in Sicily. For a long time Giorgio lived in London and Madrid. The supermarket shelves there looked similar to those in

Palermo, they reminded him of his home in Sicily. But a huge number of products were imported, whereas, in Palermo, you get everything fresh and from regional suppliers, because such a wonderful and varied array of food is produced right here.

Nowadays Giorgio is increasingly being booked as a classic city tour guide in addition to his role as a food guide. This is because more and more visitors want to explore local flavours while admiring the city's architectural attractions, both remnants of the city's multicultural past.

On these tours you walk for anything up to four hours, sometimes in the blazing sun, through the tumultuous street markets. It is physically strenuous, particularly for the guide. But people absolutely love it, and when they finish they are exhilarated by the diversity and wealth of information they've been given. It's five years since Giorgio started offering these tours. He hopes to be able to do this job for ever, or for as long as his legs will let him…

White Sicilian focaccia

Lo sfincione bianco di Bagheria

Serves 6–8
Prep 1 hr 20 mins, plus
 resting time

6g (¹⁄₄oz) fresh yeast
20g (³⁄₄oz) sugar, plus
 1½ tbsp
400g (14oz) flour (ideally
 an ancient Sicilian
 variety of wheat, such as
 Maiorca, Russello,
 Perciasacchi, or Tumminia
 (see p130); or emmer)
sea salt and freshly ground
 black pepper
6 tbsp extra virgin olive
 oil, plus more for
 drizzling
800g (1³⁄₄lb) white onions,
 sliced into rings
1 garlic clove, finely
 chopped
120ml (4fl oz) white wine
 vinegar
60g (2oz) fresh breadcrumbs,
 or *mollica fresca* (see p30)
40g (1¹⁄₂oz) pecorino cheese,
 finely grated
dried oregano
500g (1lb 2oz) young sheep's
 cheese, for instance
 Tuma and / or ricotta,
 or manouri, cut into
 1cm- (¹⁄₂in-) thick slices

Supposedly it was the nuns at the Abbey of San Vito who invented this street food, the most famous dish from Palermo and the surrounding province. *Sfincione* is a cross between pizza and focaccia. Its appeal lies in a very soft, thick layer of dough which is normally topped with just a few ingredients. The classic version is made with tomato sauce, onions, oregano, and sometimes also anchovies, and caciocavallo. This recipe comes from Bagheria. It is made without any tomatoes at all and is completely white.

Stir the yeast into 220ml (7½fl oz) of lukewarm water with the 20g (³⁄₄oz) sugar and 150g (5½oz) of the flour. Cover and leave to prove in a warm, sheltered place for 1 hour.

Mix the remaining flour with 10g (¼oz) salt. Use a food processor to knead this into your starter dough along with 3 tbsp of olive oil, for about 6 minutes. Shape into a ball, cover, and leave to prove in a warm, sheltered place for 2 hours.

Next, heat another 3 tbsp of olive oil in a sauté pan. Gently sweat the onions and garlic for 20 minutes, seasoning with salt and pepper, and stirring often. Mix the vinegar and the 1½ tbsp sugar in a small bowl, pour into the pan, and simmer gently for another 15 minutes. Remove from the heat and allow to cool.

Place a sheet of baking parchment on a thin wooden board and place a baking ring 25cm (10in) in diameter on top. Use your fingers to spread the dough out inside the ring, then cover and leave to prove for another hour.

Mix the crumbs with the pecorino, some black pepper, and oregano.

Slide a baking tray into the centre of the oven and preheat it to 220°C (425°F/Gas 7).

First spread the sheep's cheese over the dough base, then cover with the cooled onion mixture, and finish with the crumbs. Drizzle with olive oil. Carefully slide the *sfincione* – still in the baking ring and on its baking parchment – onto the baking tray. At the same time, carefully pull out the wooden board from underneath.

Bake for 20–30 minutes until the crust is golden. Leave to cool briefly, then remove the baking ring. Drizzle with olive oil to serve.

Serves 4

Prep 1 hr, plus soaking time;
start the evening before

Grilled octopus with ricotta houmous, panelle, and lemon couscous

Polpo grigliato con crema di ceci, panelle, e couscous al limone

For the ricotta houmous
250g (9oz) yellow chickpeas
80g (2¾oz) black chickpeas
1 small carrot, chopped
2 pinches bicarbonate
   of soda
2 tbsp extra virgin olive oil
1 celery stick, finely chopped
1 bay leaf
sea salt and black pepper
1 level tsp curry powder
splash of lemon juice
100g (3½oz) ricotta

For the panelle
60g (2oz) chickpea flour
40g (1½oz) "00" pasta flour
finely grated zest of
   1 organic lemon
500ml (16fl oz) neutral oil

For the couscous
200ml (7fl oz) vegetable
   stock
1 tbsp extra virgin olive oil
100g (3½oz) couscous

For the lemon sauce
100ml (3½fl oz) freshly
   squeezed lemon juice
2 garlic cloves, finely
   chopped
handful each of mint and
   parsley or oregano leaves,
   roughly torn
finely grated zest of
   1 organic lemon

500–600g (1lb 2oz–1lb 5oz)
   cooked octopus tentacles

Separately soak the yellow and black chickpeas overnight. Once you are ready to cook, drain and rinse the yellow chickpeas, then put in a saucepan with 1 litre (1¾ pints) of water, the carrot, a pinch of bicarbonate of soda, 1 tbsp of the olive oil, and celery. Cook over a medium heat for up to 2 hours, until soft. Top up the water if needed. Drain, reserving 50ml (1¾fl oz) liquid.

Drain the black chickpeas, then cook for 45 minutes in 500ml (18fl oz) of water with the bay leaf and a pinch of bicarbonate of soda, then drain.

Put the yellow chickpeas in a food processor, reserving a handful to use as a garnish. Add the carrot, salt, pepper, 1 tbsp of the olive oil, the curry powder, and lemon juice to the food processor, and blitz to a purée. If necessary, add a bit of cooking liquid. Stir this creamy mixture into the ricotta, adjust the seasoning and lemon juice, and keep warm.

To make the panelle, knead both types of flour with 3 tbsp of lukewarm water, some salt, and the lemon zest until you have a firm, homogeneous dough. Cover and leave to rest for 30 minutes.

Fill a small, high-sided saucepan around three-quarters full with neutral oil and heat to 180°C (350°F). Hold a wooden skewer in the oil to test its temperature: when small bubbles form on it, the oil is hot enough.

Roll the dough out on a lightly floured work surface until it is about 7mm (¼in) thick, stamp out shapes and fry these in batches in the hot oil until golden. Remove them with a slotted spoon and drain on kitchen paper. Season sparingly with salt and pepper, then set aside to keep warm.

For the couscous, bring the vegetable stock to the boil in a pan with the olive oil, remove from the heat, and stir in the couscous. Season with pepper and leave the grains to swell for around 20 minutes, until the stock has been absorbed.

To make the lemon sauce, mix all the ingredients together, season to taste, and fold half of it into the couscous. Fork it through to fluff up the grains.

Heat a griddle without any oil. Cook the octopus tentacles on both sides and immediately mix them with the remaining lemon sauce.

Arrange the couscous, houmous, panelle, and octopus along with the lemon sauce on 4 plates. Scatter over the black chickpeas, the reserved yellow chickpeas, and some sea salt flakes. Drizzle with a dash of olive oil to serve.

Makes about 12
Prep 1 hr 20 mins, plus
    cooling time

Arancini with tuna and aubergine

Arancini con tonno e melanzane

For the rice coating
500g (1lb 2oz) arborio rice
coarse sea salt
4 tbsp pecorino cheese,
    finely grated
4 tbsp Parmesan cheese,
    finely grated
2 tsp curry powder
100g (3½oz) fine "00" grade
    durum wheat semolina
    flour
160g (5¾oz) fine dried
    breadcrumbs, or *mollica
    secca* (see p30)

For the stuffing
extra virgin olive oil
220g (8oz) aubergines, in
    1½cm (¾in) cubes
180g (6oz) tuna fillet, in
    1½cm (¾in) cubes
sea salt and freshly ground
    black pepper
15–20g (½–¾oz) fine "00"
    grade durum wheat
    semolina flour
1 onion, sliced into strips
350g (12oz) canned chopped
    tomatoes
2 tbsp chopped basil leaves
2 tbsp chopped mint leaves
chilli flakes
100–120g (3½–4oz)
    provolone cheeese, chopped
    into 1½ cm (¾in) cubes,
    or cooking mozzarella

neutral flavoured oil,
    for deep-frying

For a long time, pretty much all you could get was *arancino al ragù* (with pieces of meat) in Catania. Traditionally, they would also have been stuffed with cheese, never with béchamel. *Arancino bianco*, which aren't really white at all, are stuffed with ham, peas, and a béchamel cheese sauce. Nowadays it's hard to keep track of all the different versions of *arancini*. But in Sicily it's important to order an "*arancino*" in Palermo and an "*arancina*" in Catania. You see, in Palermo, these little rice balls are feminine and round. The pointed male *arancini* come from Catania.

Cook the rice in 1.2 litres (2 pints) of salted water until *al dente*. While the rice is still warm (but ensuring there is no water remaining), mix it with the pecorino, Parmesan, and curry powder. Transfer to the refrigerator to chill for at least 1 hour.

To make the filling, heat a generous amount of olive oil in a pan. Fry the aubergines over a high heat, then set aside. Season the tuna sparingly with salt, toss the pieces in flour, and sauté for 1–2 minutes in olive oil.

Heat some olive oil in another pan. Sauté the onion until golden. Combine the tomatoes with 100ml (3½fl oz) of water, then stir this into the pan with the basil and mint. Season to taste with salt and chilli flakes. Allow the sauce to simmer down slightly. Spoon in the tuna and aubergine, remove from the heat, cover, and leave to cool.

Shape 1 handful of chilled rice with your hands to make a ball. Then press it in the centre to create a large cavity. Insert a good 1 tbsp of sauce and 1–2 cubes of provolone. Carefully spread the rice back over the filling and smooth it back into a ball. Make 12 little balls in the same way.

In a small bowl, stir together 100g (3½oz) flour and 200ml (7fl oz) of water until smooth, then season with pepper. Toss the rice balls first in this mixture, then in the breadcrumbs.

In a pan, heat the oil for frying to 180°C (350°F). Hold a wooden skewer in the oil to test: when little bubbles form on it, the oil is hot enough. Fry the little rice balls until golden brown. Drain on kitchen paper and serve warm.

Makes 6
Prep 2 hrs, plus 4 hrs
    resting time

Sicilian brioche burgers

Sicilian burger col tuppo

For the filling
6 *polpette di melanzane con
    scamorza e menta* (see p176)
¹/₃ portion *broccoli affogati*
    (see p176)
1 tbsp extra virgin olive oil
sea salt and freshly ground
    black pepper
150g (5¹/₂oz) ricotta
some basil leaves

For the brioche buns
6g (¹/₈oz) fresh yeast
420g (15oz) "00" pasta flour
200ml (7fl oz) whole milk,
    plus 1 tbsp
50ml (1³/₄fl oz) freshly
    squeezed orange juice
zest of ¹/₂ small organic
    orange
a few drops of orange oil
1 medium egg, plus 1 small
    egg yolk
70g (2¹/₄oz) caster sugar
50g (1³/₄oz) soft unsalted
    butter, chopped
¹/₂ tsp sea salt
black sesame seeds

This brioche is a nice Sicilian creation, but not every region makes them with the little "head" on top. Tourists rave about brioche with ice cream, but many Sicilians prefer to eat it for breakfast with a bowl of granita, and these buns also make great burger holders. Just sprinkle some sesame seeds on the bun and add a savoury filling.

Prepare the aubergine balls and broccoli (see p176), then set aside to keep warm.

To make the buns, dissolve the yeast in 20ml (¾fl oz) of lukewarm water.

In a saucepan, stir 20g (¾oz) of the flour with 100ml (3½fl oz) of the milk over a medium heat until you have a flexible mixture. Remove from the heat and leave to cool.

Use a food processor to briefly knead this cooled mixture together with the remaining flour, the dissolved yeast and liquid, the remaining milk, the orange juice, zest, and orange oil. Then add the whole egg and continue kneading briefly. Sprinkle in the sugar, add the butter piece by piece, and knead in the salt. Continue kneading the dough for 6–10 minutes until it is stretchy. Cover the bowl with a cloth and leave the dough to prove in a warm place for 2 hours.

Line a baking tray with baking parchment. Lightly flour a work surface and split the dough into

12 pieces (six x 100–110g / 3½–4oz, six x 20–30g / ¾–1oz). Shape each of the pieces into a ball. Place the larger balls generously spaced out on the baking tray. Make an indentation in the centre of each and place a smaller ball in each cavity. Now slide into the switched-off oven and leave the dough to prove for another 2 hours with the door closed.

Remove the tray from the oven and preheat it to 170°C (340°F/Gas 3½).

Beat the egg yolk with the 1 tbsp milk and brush each bun with this glaze. Sprinkle with sesame seeds. Bake the buns for 25–30 minutes until golden. If the little "heads" start to become too dark, cover them with foil.

Leave the buns to cool before slicing them open. Stir 1 tbsp olive oil, salt, and pepper into the ricotta. Spread 2 tbsp of this mixture onto the base of each burger bun. Arrange on the broccoli and top with 2 aubergine balls and some basil leaves.

Makes 1 loaf
Prep 1 hr 20 mins, plus
resting time; "mother"
dough (starter): 10 days

Sourdough bread with an Italian "mother"

Pane con lievito madre

For the "mother"
1.1kg (2¹/₂lb) organic flour
(ideally an old variety
such as Tumminia,
Perciasacchi, Russello,
or Maiorc, (see p130); or
emmer flour)
¹/₂ tsp honey

For the bread dough
200g (7oz) fine durum wheat
semolina flour
200g (7oz) organic flour
(ideally an old variety
such as Tumminia,
Perciasacchi, Russello,
or Maiorca, (see p130); or
emmer flour), plus extra
for dusting
100g (3¹/₂oz) "mother"

For the emulsion
12g (¹/₄oz) sea salt
20g (³/₄oz) mild, moderately
fruity olive oil (I use
Tonda Iblea), plus extra
to serve

To make the "mother", knead 100g (3½oz) of the flour with the honey and 50ml (1¾fl oz) of lukewarm water until you have a smooth dough. Shape into a ball and use a sharp knife to slice a cross in the top (don't cut all the way through). Transfer to a glass bowl, cover with a damp kitchen towel (not cling film!), and leave to prove for 48 hours in a warm, sheltered place. Keep the kitchen towel damp.

Feed and replenish the dough for at least 10 days in total. To do this, knead 100g (3½oz) of the mother dough (use the innermost part) with 100g (3½oz) flour and 50ml (1¾fl oz) of lukewarm water until you have a smooth dough. Shape this and leave to prove as described above. Repeat this process 3 more times until a total of 10 days have passed.

On the 10th day, feed the "mother" dough as usual and leave it covered to prove in a warm place for 3 hours, then transfer to the refrigerator for 12 hours.

On the 11th day (the day when you will bake the bread), take 100g (3½oz) of the "mother" dough from the refrigerator and leave it out to come to room temperature for 1 hour. Leave the rest of the "mother" in the refrigerator until the next baking day, remembering to feed it once a week as described above.

To make the bread, mix both types of flour with 350ml (12fl oz) of lukewarm water in a bowl. Cover with a kitchen towel and leave to prove for 1 hour. Then use a food processor to knead this together with the mother dough on a medium setting for 6–7 minutes.

To make the emulsion, mix all the ingredients with 40ml (1½fl oz) of lukewarm water. Knead this gradually into the dough, allowing it to absorb the liquid before pouring in more emulsion. Then knead for 5 minutes.

Cover with a damp kitchen towel and leave to prove for 5 hours in a warm, sheltered place. Carefully knead the dough into a ball on a lightly floured work surface. Transfer this ball into a well-floured proving basket, cover, and leave to rest for another 2 hours.

Place a cast-iron pan with a lid on the lowest shelf in the oven and preheat to 240°C (475°F/Gas 9), or as high as it will go.

Place the loaf on a sheet of baking parchment and transfer the bread on this and into the cast-iron pan. Close the lid. Reduce the temperature to 220°C (425°F/Gas 7) and bake for 45 minutes. Remove the lid and continue baking for 15 minutes. Leave to cool on a wire rack, then slice, and serve with olive oil and salt.

Serves 4
Prep 30 mins

Two kinds of sandwich, traditional and modern

*Pani cunsatu anticu e
pani cunsatu mudernu*

4 bread rolls or 1 large loaf,
such as foccacia or
cuccidatu Siciliano
extra virgin olive oil
sea salt and freshly ground
black pepper
chilli flakes

For a traditional sandwich
8 anchovies in salt, rinsed
16 sun-dried cherry tomatoes
in oil, or 8 regular
sun-dried tomatoes in oil
12 black olives, pitted
80–100g (2³⁄₄–3¹⁄₂oz)
pecorino cheese, finely
sliced
rosemary sprigs
dried oregano

For a modern sandwich
8 anchovies in oil
20 sun-dried cherry tomatoes
in oil, or 8–10 regular
sun-dried tomatoes in oil
20 black olives, pitted
80–100g (2³⁄₄–3¹⁄₂oz)
provolone cheese, sliced
80–100g (2³⁄₄–3¹⁄₂oz)
mozzarella, torn
8 aubergine slices, fried
4 cherry tomatoes, quartered
20 large capers
¹⁄₂ red chilli, chopped
basil leaves
dried oregano

Pani cunsatu is a sandwich, which sounds rather unexciting, but is a real phenomenon that has taken hold on the island. *Pani cunsatu* has become a cult dish in Sicily, even though it's essentially a very simple thing, which has poverty to thank for its existence. In the past, having toppings on your bread would have been considered a luxury. So if all you had was olive oil and salt, you would have just eaten your bread with those. Nowadays, modern *pani cunsati* are laden with so many toppings you can hardly see the bread underneath. Someone who has really mastered the art, and who has made a real name for himself for it, is Alfredo from the island of Salina. His pub is always absolutely rammed and his *pani cunsati* are best-sellers, along with the granita he serves.

Slice open the bread rolls, or the loaf, drizzle generously with olive oil and arrange your chosen topping ingredients as desired. Sprinkle with sea salt and herbs, then season with pepper or chilli flakes, or both. Put the other half of the rolls or loaf on top.

If you used a single large loaf, slice it into 4 equal portions to serve.

You can also heat the bread, if you like. To do this, either heat it in the oven before filling, or toast the halved bread in a pan. Or preheat the oven to 220°C (425°F/Gas 7), bake the filled rolls for 10–12 minutes, and serve warm.

LA TERRA

Sicilians are surrounded by the sea but also connected with the earth. Liquid and solid elements come together on this island. This understanding of nature makes Sicilians excellent farmers, or *terroni*, literally "connected with the earth". You would be right to think that this is a quality to be proud of.

But *terroni* is also an insult, a slur, a denigration hurled in the face of southern Italians by their northern countrymen. Sicilians have got used to being considered second-class Italian citizens. In the (materially) rich north they struggle to comprehend the paradoxical laws of nature and that's why many northerners cannot understand why Sicilians are so proud to be *terroni*. And their pride in the land is driving a return to the old ways, to a simpler time, and to *cucina povera*, literally "food of the poor".

In Barrafranca, in the heart of the Sicilian hinterland, 39 kilometres (24 miles) south west of Enna, you will find the home and workplace of the Amore family. They work with the earth and for the earth. They have gone back to the past in order to take a step forwards towards Sicily's future. And although this family farming business has existed for almost 60 years, they have formed a new, forward-looking company. Its name is SeMiniAmo.

Three years ago the business was taken over by Davide, the youngest member of the family, who is now 29. With his degree in economics, marketing, and commercial strategy, he has changed the company's direction. He has opted for the cultivation of ancient Sicilian grain varieties (*grani antichi Siciliani*), which are becoming increasingly popular on the island. It all began with a desire to respect the land, and this led to the cultivation of varietals of wheat that are traditional to this area, types that existed before the economic boom and which were forced to give way to other cultivars with the advent of intensive farming. The old Sicilian grain varieties being harvested by this young company have wonderful names: Tumminia; Perciasacchi; Russello; Maiorca. They also contain high-quality nutrients.

Why would you take what seems to be a step backwards, choosing a path that involves more work and less money? Davide's motivations are wide-ranging, as he explains: "The cultivation of old grains is not just a crucial factor for biodiversity, it's also a question of quality. We know about this fabulous, healthy raw material, one of only very few. It has escaped genetic modification by humans, it is in harmony with natural cycles, and it thrives without the use of chemical fertilizers. Our grain has exceptional nutritional properties, the gluten is less tough and elastic, so it is easier for our digestive system to handle." That all makes sense, but this grain is nowhere near as profitable as the other (over-) cultivated varieties the western world has grown used to.

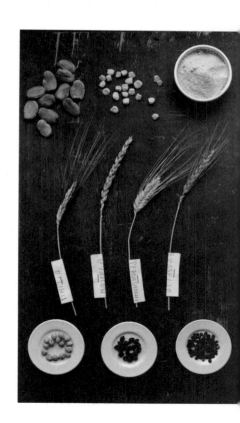

Davide explains: "We made a choice to grow ancient grains. For us, this was an ethical decision rather than a commercial one. It means we can respect nature and its biodiversity, plus it's beneficial for human health. We use our ancient grains to produce pasta, which is extruded using bronze dies and dried slowly at low temperatures. Our flour is ground on natural stone. To retain the quality and authenticity of the ancient grains, the production process must preserve all the exceptional properties of this wheat, creating healthy products with an unmistakable flavour. It is gratifying to know that we are introducing families to genuine, healthy products which evoke the flavours of the past. And it's even more pleasing that these products are being created with the greatest respect for the planet on which we live. Our entire approach is based on sustainable farming, an ethical business model, and high-quality products. And we believe this is the only possible choice if we want to face the future with a clear conscience. As we are fond of saying: there can be no future without the past."

In addition to the four ancient wheat varieties, which are used to make flour and pasta (*penne*, *busiate*, *maccheroni*, *fusilli*, and *ditalini*), the family also produces almonds, almond butter, and two kinds of chickpeas: black *ceci neri* and white *ceci pascià*. These are chickpeas with an intense flavour and a high proportion of minerals, best enjoyed with just some sea salt and fine olive oil, like all high-quality products, to be honest. The family also produces black lentils from Leonforte. That's where I head to find out more about the town's renowned broad beans.

The town of Leonforte was founded in 1610 by Prince Nicolo Placido Branciforte and is located 18 kilometres (11 miles) north-east of Enna. It is famous for the Granfonte (better known as the Fontana dei 24 Cannoli, see photograph, p135), a wonderful cattle trough built in the Sicilian Baroque style. But the town is also known for its very large, flat broad beans, or *fava*. The *fava larga di Leonforte* have been included in the Slow Food movement's Ark of Taste.

In the past, broad beans were cultivated in alternating cycles with wheat, and they have always been a traditional ingredient in kitchens in Leonforte.

The fresh beans are harvested in late March or early April and are served raw, scattered with pecorino cheese, or cooked into *frittedda* or *pitaggiu* (see p35). Dried broad beans are available from mid-July and these are used for the popular dish *maccu* (see p134). In contrast to other varieties, they do not require extensive soaking and they cook more quickly.

The *fava larga di Leonforte*, also referred to by the town's inhabitants as *fava turca* (Turkish bean), is the largest bean in Italy and in the past it would have been served alongside grains as "the poor person's meat". The high protein content in these broad beans can compensate for the lack of protein in a person's diet from animal products. The beans also keep well as a dried product, and travel well.

Almost all the products that featured in *cucina povera* were fundamentally healthier than those found in the cuisine of the rich. This just wasn't appreciated in the past, when people always aspired to mimic the culinary habits of the wealthy. Nowadays, we have a better understanding, and are looking back to the past to re-evaluate these valuable food treasures.

Broad bean purée with black olives, chicory, and toast

Maccu con olive nere, cicoria, e pane brustolito

For the purée

2–3 tbsp extra virgin olive oil (I use Nocellara Etnea or Verdello for this)

1 onion, finely chopped

1 large garlic clove, finely chopped

100g (3½oz) carrot, finely chopped

a few wild fennel sprigs, or dill with fennel seeds

1 celery stick, finely chopped

400g (14oz) podded, dried broad beans

250g (9oz) floury potatoes, peeled and finely chopped

sea salt and freshly ground black pepper

For the chicory

1kg (2lb 4oz) chicory, or endives, dandelion, or Swiss chard

coarse sea salt

2 tbsp extra virgin olive oil, plus extra to serve

1 large garlic clove, sliced

16–20 black olives, pitted

1 red chilli, finely chopped

4 large slices of white bread, toasted

This purée is really popular all over the south of Italy, with just minor variations in the recipe from place to place. Here, I use *fava larga* from Leonforte (see p132). Other varieties can also be used, of course! *Maccu* can also be fried: let it go completely cold until it solidifies, then slice and cook, as you would polenta. Transform this bean purée into a classic *aperitivo Siciliano* by spreading it on bread then topping things off with fresh figs and pistachios, or grapes and basil, or aubergine and *ricotta salata* (see photo bottom right).

Put the olive oil in a large pan over a medium heat. Sauté the onion, garlic, carrot, wild fennel, and celery.

Add the broad beans and potatoes, then pour in enough water to cover everything by about 4cm (1½in). With the lid half on, cook until the beans and potatoes are very soft, stirring often and topping up with boiling water as soon as it has been absorbed. After about 45 minutes, season well. The beans should be soft like a purée. If you like, you can press this bean purée through a coarse sieve to make it smoother. Set aside and keep warm.

Trim the woody ends from the stalks of chicory and make a wedge-shaped incision in the base of the leaves. Split the leaves and stalks separately into large pieces. Get a bowl filled with iced water ready.

Blanch the stalks in a generous quantity of boiling, salted water for about 5 minutes, then add the leaves and continue cooking for another 4 minutes. Immerse the chicory in the iced water at the end of this cooking time. Drain and squeeze any remaining liquid out by hand.

Gently heat the olive oil in a large pan and sauté the garlic and olives until golden, then briefly toss in the chicory. Season to taste with salt and chilli.

Arrange the bean purée on 4 plates, top with chicory and olives, drizzle with plenty of oil, and serve with toast.

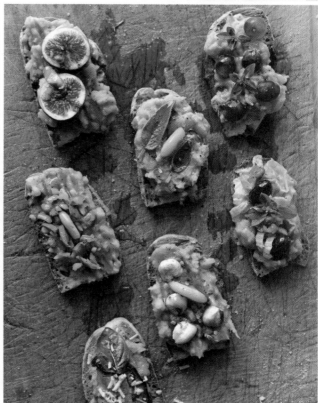

Broad beans with tomatoes and fried egg

Fave con pomodori e uovo fritto

400g (14oz) fresh or frozen
   broad beans, podded
coarse sea salt
4 tbsp extra virgin olive
   oil, plus extra for frying
   and drizzling
2 spring onions with large
   bulbs, white sections
   only, sliced
1 large garlic clove,
   finely chopped
1kg (2lb 4oz) tomatoes,
   ideally datterini or
   cherry tomatoes, fresh or
   canned, stalks removed,
   and quartered
1 tbsp vincotto (cooked
   grape must), or 1 tbsp
   syrup
2 handfuls of basil leaves
sea salt
chilli flakes
8 eggs

These three ingredients came together by chance in our kitchen in Sicily. So there is no long Sicilian tradition involved here, even if there are Persian influences at play. I used frozen broad beans to cook this recipe because, sadly, fresh broad beans are only in season for a very short time, which makes the frozen variety a good option.

Blanch the broad beans for 1–2 minutes in plenty of boiling, salted water, then remove with a slotted spoon and immerse in iced water to prevent further cooking. Slip off the tough outer skins to reveal the bright green bean beneath.

Heat the olive oil in a large saucepan. Sauté the onions and garlic, then add the tomatoes, vincotto, and half the basil. Season everything with salt and chilli flakes and braise for about 5 minutes. Add the broad beans and continue cooking for 10 minutes. If the sauce becomes too thick, add a bit of hot water. Season with salt. Remove the pan from the heat and set aside to keep warm.

If you are making half the quantity because there are fewer people (or if you are eating the dish as an intermediate course), you can fry the eggs in the same pan. To do this, push the vegetables to the side of the pan, pour in some extra olive oil, and fry the eggs. If you are making the full recipe quantity with 8 eggs, fry them separately in another pan.

Finally, scoop the bean and tomato mixture onto 4 plates, arrange 2 fried eggs in the centre of each and drizzle with olive oil. Scatter with the remaining basil leaves and some sea salt to serve.

Double Jerusalem artichoke with black lentils and crispy chicken feet

Topinambur con lenticchie nere e zampa di gallina

For the stock
4 chicken feet, ready to cook
1 celery stick, chopped
1/2 bunch parsley, chopped
1 carrot, chopped
1 white onion, chopped
2 garlic cloves, chopped
4 cloves
2 bay leaves
sea salt and freshly ground
   red Kampot pepper

For the lentils
200g (7oz) black lentils, or
   brown lentils
1 small organic orange,
   1 strip of pared zest,
   the remaining zest
   finely grated
extra virgin olive oil

For the Jerusalem artichokes
800g (1³/₄lb) organic
   Jerusalem artichokes
400g (14oz) floury potatoes,
   peeled and chopped
1 large garlic clove, chopped
100ml (3¹/₂fl oz) milk
70ml (2¹/₂fl oz) white wine
freshly grated nutmeg

To finish the dish
extra virgin olive oil
plain flour, for coating
good handful of pine nuts,
   toasted (optional)
herbs of your choice

Jerusalem artichoke has been around in Sicily for ages, and yet there are hardly any recipes for it. This dish boasts Jerusalem artichoke cooked in two different ways with contrasting textures. The stock for the Jerusalem artichoke purée is prepared with the chicken feet, which you then fry and serve alongside. This is another ancient ingredient that Sicilian cooks would previously have served as a matter of course and now is being rediscovered — albeit as yet on a relatively small scale.

To make the stock, pour 1.5 litres (2³/₄ pints) of water into a large saucepan, add all the ingredients and season with salt. Simmer over a medium heat for 45 minutes, then strain through a sieve. Set aside the stock and chicken feet separately. Discard the vegetables.

Meanwhile, rinse the lentils in a sieve. Cook them for 30 minutes in a saucepan with 800ml (1¹/₄ pints) of water and the pared strip of orange zest until *al dente*. Drain and discard the orange zest, then season and toss in olive oil.

Meanwhile, clean the Jerusalem artichokes and finely slice 120g (4¹/₄oz) of them, unpeeled. Peel the rest of the Jerusalem artichokes and cut into cubes. Put the cubed Jerusalem artichoke into a saucepan with the potatoes, garlic, milk, wine, and 1 litre (1³/₄ pints) of the stock. Season with salt, pepper, and nutmeg and cook over a medium heat until the potatoes are tender. Mash them and adjust the seasoning, then press through a fine sieve. Set aside to keep warm.

Dab the chicken feet dry and toss in flour to coat. Heat a generous quantity of olive oil in a pan and fry the chicken feet until crisp. Then fry the Jerusalem artichoke slices in the oil and transfer to kitchen paper to absorb the fat.

Segment the flesh of the orange between the membranes and chop into small pieces.

Serve the purée on 4 plates and arrange the lentils and Jerusalem artichoke slices on top. Finish with a chicken foot and some orange segments. Scatter with orange zest, season with red pepper, sprinkle over some salt, and drizzle with olive oil. If desired, scatter with toasted pine nuts, and herbs of your choice.

Intermezzi

Serves 4
Prep 25–40 mins (depending
   on the type of bean), plus
   soaking and drying time;
   start the previous day

Fried broad beans

Fave fritte

300g (10oz) dried broad
   beans, ideally skinned
500ml (16fl oz) neutral
   flavoured oil, for frying
sea salt and freshly ground
   black pepper, or chilli
   flakes
your choice of herbs,
   shredded, as desired
your choice of spices
   (see bottom right)

At Sicilian markets you will find all kinds of dried pulses, including some you can eat straight away as a snack or *aperitivo Siciliano* (see p223). You might like to buy some *ciciri e favi caliati* (chickpeas and fava beans cooked in the embers). These pulses are traditionally eaten at parties, although you need good teeth to cope with them! There are two ways to prepare softer fried fava beans: they can be fried in their skins, which are called *fave fritte in camicia* ("fried broad beans in their shirts"), or peeled and fried in halves (as shown here), known simply as *fave fritte*. I strongly caution against attempting to make your own "beans in shirts" at home! The beans can literally explode in the hot oil if they are not absolutely 100 per cent dry, or if a bit of air is trapped inside the skin.

Cover the broad beans with plenty of water and leave to soak for 24 hours. Drain. If they are still in their skins, use a knife to pull these off and slice the beans in half or, if they are already peeled, dry the beans very carefully. Ideally this should be done in a food dehydrator, otherwise dry them very thoroughly, then leave them spread out in the air for at least 1 hour.

Fill a high-sided pan one-third full with the oil for frying and heat this to at least 170°C (340°F) but no higher than 180°C (350°F). To test, hold a wooden skewer in the oil; you should barely see any little bubbles forming.

Fry the dried beans in very small portions until golden. Scoop them out with a slotted spoon and transfer to kitchen paper to drain. Season with salt, pepper, or chilli flakes while they are still hot. Mix with herbs or spices as desired. Enjoy them as a snack, or serve as an *aperitivo Siciliano* (see p223).

My favourite spice mix: sea salt flakes, smoked paprika, sage, thyme, and freshly ground black pepper or chilli flakes.

Smoked tuna with grilled aubergine, figs, burrata, and a hint of orange

Tonno affumicato con melanzana grigliata, fichi, burrata, e profumo d'arancia

sea salt and freshly ground
　black pepper
2 medium aubergines, stalks
　removed, cut into 7mm-
　(¹/₄in-) thick slices
8–12 slices of smoked tuna
4 balls of burrata
8 figs, quartered
red and green basil leaves
pinch of finely grated zest
　from 1 organic orange
extra virgin olive oil

The inspiration for this dish was the hugely popular Italian antipasto *prosciutto crudo, fichi, e burrata*. I kept the burrata and figs but, for the Sicilian version, I replaced the *prosciutto crudo* with smoked tuna and aubergines. Needless to say, I couldn't resist smuggling in my favourite ingredient: orange. It complements the aubergine and tuna beautifully.

Lightly salt the aubergines and cook on both sides in a hot griddle pan without any oil.

On 4 plates, arrange alternate slices of aubergine and tuna in a fan pattern, using 2 or 3 slices of each.

Place a ball of burrata alongside. Add the quartered figs.

Scatter over both types of basil and some sea salt, add a touch of orange zest, season with pepper, and drizzle lightly with olive oil to serve.

Makes about 24
Prep 35 mins, plus resting
and cooling time

Mini sesame panini with lemon marmalade and scamorza

Panini al sesamo con marmellata di limone e scamorza

For the sesame rolls
1 portion Mafalda dough
  (see p148)
a little whole milk
3 tbsp sesame seeds

For the topping
200g (7oz) lemon marmalade
12 mini scamorza balls
1 organic lemon, orange,
  or lime, thinly sliced
  and quartered

Sesame is a popular ingredient in Sicilian bread baking. It is also used to make one of the most traditional sweet treats, the *giuggiulena*. This is a type of *torrone* (similar to nougat) made from sesame and honey, and with clear Arabic influences. In Ispica, a town in the province of Ragusa, they cultivate dark, amber-coloured sesame seeds, which are endorsed by Slow Food. Two older farmers have protected this variety against manipulation by the seed industry by repeatedly sowing the extremely ancient seeds. In terms of their nutritional properties, these seeds are far superior to those used in industrial farming.

To make the mini sesame panini, prepare the dough (see p148). After the first 3 hours of proving, make 24 little balls from the dough.

Brush the mini panini with milk and scatter with sesame seeds.

Line 1 or 2 baking trays with baking parchment and leave the panini to prove for an hour on the trays in a switched-off oven.

Remove from the oven and preheat to 220°C (425°F/Gas 7). Slide the tray back into the centre of the oven. Spray the walls of the oven with water, reduce the temperature to 200°C (400°F/Gas 6) and bake the panini for 10–15 minutes until they begin to colour slightly.

Leave to cool completely under a tea towel. Cut each one open and fill with some lemon marmalade, a ball of scamorza, and a quarter of a citrus slice. Best served with an aperitivo (see p223).

Makes 4
Prep 1 hr 10 mins, plus
    resting and cooling time

Sicilian sesame rolls with mortadella

Mafalda con mortadella

For the dough
6g (¹/₄oz) fresh yeast
150g (5¹/₂oz) fine "00" grade
    durum wheat semolina
    flour, plus extra for
    dusting
pinch of sugar
350g (12oz) fine durum wheat
    semolina (*semola di grano
    duro rimacinata*)
2 tbsp olive oil
10g (¹/₄oz) sea salt
1–2 tbsp milk
3 tbsp black and / or white
    sesame seeds

For the topping
8–12 wafer-thin slices
    of Sicilian mortadella
    with pistachios

Mortadella is famously associated with Bologna, but it used to be really popular in Sicily too, thanks to being inexpensive as well as incredibly tasty. *Mafalda con mortadella* is a classic Sicilian dish. Mafalda is a type of bread that most Sicilians remember fondly from childhood, because it makes such a convenient snack. Although Mafalda is primarily linked with the province of Palermo, history tells us that it was a master baker from Catania who dedicated this bread to Princess Mafalda of Savoy in the early 20th century.

First make the starter dough by kneading the yeast with 20g (³/₄oz) of the flour by hand to a crumbly consistency. Dissolve this mixture in 50ml (1³/₄fl oz) of lukewarm water and the pinch of sugar. Cover with a damp tea towel and leave to prove for 1 hour in a warm, sheltered place.

Meanwhile, for the water roux, put 20g (³/₄oz) more of the flour into a saucepan with 100ml (3½fl oz) of water and heat, stirring constantly. Once the consistency is gelatinous, cook for 2 more minutes, continuing to stir. Leave to cool completely.

Knead both of these starter mixtures into the remaining flour, the durum wheat semolina, 200 ml (7fl oz) of lukewarm water, and the olive oil for 6–8 minutes until you have a smooth dough. Gradually add the salt as you work. Cover the dough with a damp tea towel and leave to prove in a warm, sheltered place for at least 3 hours.

Divide the dough into quarters and roll each of these out on a floured work surface to create a strand measuring about 60cm (24in). Shape each of these like a snake, twisting the strands back and forth 3 times and placing the final strand on top (see photos, right). Brush lightly with milk and sprinkle with sesame seeds. Line a baking tray with baking parchment. Leave the rolls to prove on the tray for 1 hour in a switched-off oven.

Remove from the oven and preheat to 220°C (425°F/Gas 7). Slide the tray into the lower part of the oven. Spray the walls of the oven with water, reduce the temperature to 200°C (400°F/Gas 6) and bake for 10–15 minutes. Then continue cooking on the middle shelf for another 15–20 minutes until they get some colour.

Leave to cool completely under a tea towel. Slice them open, fill with 2 or 3 slices of mortadella and serve.

Courgette flowers stuffed with Italian sausages and mozzarella with a pistachio coating

Fiori di zucchini ripieni con salsiccia, mozzarella in crosta di pistacchi

For the courgette flowers

10 courgette or squash flowers

2 medium eggs

sea salt and freshly ground black pepper

15g (½oz) pecorino cheese, finely grated

15g (½oz) pistachios, finely chopped

50g (1¾oz) fine dried breadcrumbs, or *mollica secca* (see p30)

For the stuffing

100g (3½oz) Italian fennel sausages (*salsiccia al finocchietto*), or coarsely ground pork mixed with fennel seeds

100g (3½oz) mozzarella, chopped into 10 cubes

extra virgin olive oil

When I published my first recipes using courgette or squash flowers, eating these wonderful blooms was a practice virtually unknown in the rest of Europe. Nowadays, you can even find them in supermarkets. Of course, anyone with a garden can have access to their own fresh supply. And if you harvest more than you know what to do with, they can be frozen.

Carefully clean the flowers. The inner flower pistil is edible, but some people find it too bitter. So, if you prefer, you can remove the pistil with your fingernails. Trim the stalk at its base.

To make the coating, beat the eggs with some salt and pepper in a deep dish. In a separate deep dish, combine the pecorino, pistachios, and breadcrumbs, mixing them well.

Preheat the oven to 200°C (400°F/ Gas 6). Line a baking tray with baking parchment.

To make the stuffing, squeeze the sausagemeat out of its skin and shape it into 10 equal-sized balls. Carefully open the flowers using your fingers and insert a ball of sausage and a mozzarella cube into each one. Then gently press the ends of the petals together to close them.

Coat the stuffed flowers, first in the egg mixture, then in the pistachio mixture. Lay the coated flowers on the prepared tray.

Drizzle the flowers with a dash of olive oil and bake in the centre of the oven for 15–20 minutes. Serve warm.

SALVATORE

Graniti is a little village with just 1,500 inhabitants
in the Alcantara valley. In the early 1960s, the village
experienced a massive exodus. Young people had no work, so
they headed north to the mainland. Some stayed in Milan,
others in Turin, others still headed to Switzerland, and
Germany, or even to England in search of a better life.
Nowadays the younger generation have no desire to leave.
They are looking for ways to build a future for themselves
here in Sicily. They love their village.

Graniti itself has always had artistic tendencies, and its
people are receptive to culture. Sculptors such as Giuseppe
Mazzullo and his godson Pippo Mannino were born here,
spent some of their childhood in the village, and also
worked here at various times. On the first weekend in
August, there is a festival in honour of San Sebastiano,
the village saint. The entire village is permeated by
the aroma of macaroni with salsa, served by *le mamme*.
Everyone gets together to have a great party and the
village comes to life.

Kochbuch
Slow Food
E 15.-

Sardellen Bio
E 5.50

Salsa Carbonella
E 5.-

Salvatore Romano's Sicilian parents had been living in Switzerland for a long time when his mother decided that Salvatore should be born on home soil rather than abroad. So she and her husband travelled to Sicily, to Graniti in the province of Messina, where she opted for a home birth to bring her son into the world. Then she returned with him to Switzerland. When he was nine, his father died. And when his older brother moved out, he was left living alone with his mother. At the same time, aged 11, his love of cooking began to emerge. In part this was because he was a typical latchkey kid who had to cook for himself. He embarked on all sorts of culinary experiments with his friend Rosario, some of which resulted in the odd saucepan having to be thrown away. Time with his mother was mostly limited to Saturdays and Sundays, and these hours would be spent cooking together. It was his mother who impressed on him the lesson that quality was far more important than quantity in food, even though Italian ingredients were particularly expensive in Switzerland. As Salvatore recalls: "We only bought them once a month, but we were happier spending money on these items than on other things. Our Italian supplies had to be used pretty sparingly, but what little we had was at least extremely good."

However, he did not train as a chef (even though that was his greatest wish), because his cousin Francesco was already training as a chef in Germany, so he felt he couldn't do that too. He considered his other options. Since he also loved technology, he decided to become an IT system administrator. Then, in 2002, he met Karin from Switzerland. The two of them also discovered a mutual love of food. So in late 2003 he decided to have a complete career change. It was too late to train as a chef, but he wanted to work in some other way with food.

However, in 2004, a life-threatening virus tore through Switzerland, and Salvatore, who was already weakened by a cold, succumbed to this illness. He was put into an artificial coma for ten days. After that, everything changed. "Now I have to do what I've always wanted to do. Now it's time to do something we are really passionate about," he said to Karin afterwards. So Salvatore and Karin opened a little bar near Basel. One year later, they added a delicatessen, dedicated to Italian specialities. They travelled all over Italy researching their product range. In Sicily they came to the conclusion that the raw produce on sale was by far the best they had found. So, in addition to the bar and delicatessen, they rented a factory. Here they manufactured the first products of their own. They started with just three items: *crema di pomodoro* (tomato spread), *carciofata* (artichoke spread) and *crema di peperoncino* (chilli spread). These homemade products always sold out immediately, so production grew and grew. Eventually, a restaurant serving Mediterranean food was added to the bar and delicatessen.

The decision to return to Sicily full time was made by Karin. After a strenuous Christmas trading season, they would wrap up a bottle of prosecco and a panettone and take the train down from Basel to Sicily. The whole of January would be spent relaxing in Salvatore's birth village: Graniti. These stays began gradually becoming longer and longer. The lifestyle in Sicily, the vegetation, the chaos, the people: Karin loved all of it. The yearning for Sicily steadily intensified. So they sold up everything in Switzerland and moved to Sicily with just a couple of suitcases and a food processor. Karin renovated the house where Salvatore was born and refurbished everything. This is where they now live and work.

At first, they rented out holiday apartments and continued making homemade products under the brand name Tasting Sicily. Salvatore is now a creative in the food industry. His style is partially influenced by *cucina dei Monsù* (see p86): elements from conquistador cuisine are combined with other components to create a new

interpretation of existing traditions. The idea that "this is the recipe and that's the way it has to stay" is something he finds ridiculous. He is absolutely convinced that you can take a traditional cuisine like that of Sicily and continue to develop it into something new.

Since 2014, they have also added artistic projects, led by Karin as a kind of artist in residence. The couple provide artists with a place to both live and work. And the Graniti *Murales* street art project attracts artists from all over the world, who travel here to paint designated façades in the village. No doubt the future holds plenty of other projects for Karin and Salvatore. Before I leave Graniti, Salvatore puts me in touch with Gaetano Marchetta, who supplies him with capers from the Aeolian island of Salina for use in his culinary creations (see p75).

Salvatore Romano's recipes depend on the high quality of the products used, the principle he learned from cooking with his mother all those years ago. They are unfussy and easy to make. That's why I have transcribed the four recipes that follow pretty much in their original form, just as they would be familiar to Italians. The instructions consist of descriptive text, without precise quantities. If you use good-quality ingredients, you can't go wrong with dishes as simple as these, even without weighing scales. All that's needed for success is a pinch of courage, a willingness to experiment, and some confidence.

Potatoes cooked in sea water, by Salvatore Romano

Patate fritte all'acqua di mare

waxy organic potatoes
sea water, or highly salted
  water
extra virgin olive oil
rosemary sprigs
1 garlic clove, crushed

In all his recipes, Salvatore uses his own olive oil (Kore), which was awarded two gold stars in Britain's 2018 Great Taste Awards. This olive oil uses a blend of Moresca and Biancolilla olives.

Clean the potatoes and slice them first into roughly 5mm- (¼in-) thick discs, then into batons. Cover with sea water in a bowl and leave to stand for 20 minutes.

Cook the potatoes in the sea water until *just* done.

Drain the sea water and gently finish cooking the potatoes in olive oil in a large pan with some rosemary sprigs and crushed garlic until they are slightly crisp.

Sicilian olive oil varieties:

Tonda Iblea, Nocellara del Belice, Biancolilla, Cerasuola, Nocellara Etnea, Verdello, and Moresca are among the best-known, though there are many more.

Serves 2
Prep 15 mins, plus chilling
and marinating time

Tuna tartare marinated in sea water and served with red prawns, by Salvatore Romano

Tàrtara di tonno marinato all'acqua di mare con gambero rosso

200g (7oz) very fresh tuna
80ml (2³/₄fl oz) sea water, or
   highly salted water
juice and some of the finely
   grated zest from
   1¹/₂ organic lemons
¹/₂ small mild red chilli,
   finely chopped
some mint leaves, finely
   shredded
1 garlic clove, finely
   chopped
extra virgin olive oil
sea salt and freshly ground
   black pepper
2 fresh red prawns
   (*gamberi rossi*)

These prawns are fished in late summer and can also be bought frozen. The fishermen place great importance on rapidly freezing the prawns as soon as they are caught, to preserve their taste, appearance, and texture. Salvatore makes this with swordfish (as shown) but tuna works equally well for this recipe.

Freeze the tuna until it is semi-frozen. Then chop finely with a large knife and gently mix with the sea water, some lemon juice and zest, chilli, mint, garlic, and olive oil, plus some freshly ground black pepper. Cover with cling film and leave to marinate in the refrigerator for about 30 minutes. (If you prefer, you can add the zest shortly before serving.)

Meanwhile, peel and devein the prawns. Salvatore uses a toothpick to lift up the intestinal tract, then it is easy to pull out. Dab the prawns dry and place them in a bowl with some freshly squeezed lemon juice (the prawns should not be totally submerged) and a pinch of salt, then leave to marinate briefly, turning them 2–3 times during the marinating process.

Remove the fish tartare from the refrigerator and pour away any liquid that has been exuded. Place a metal ring on each serving plate, fill each with half the tartare and press down gently. Remove the ring, arrange the prawn on the tartare and drizzle with olive oil.

Gamberi rossi:

In Mazara del Vallo in Trapani province, an exceptionally high-quality red prawn is caught, which has achieved worldwide fame under the name Rosso di Mazara. These prawns live at a depth of up to 700 metres (766 yards). Due to evaporation levels in the Mediterranean, the prawns are enriched with minerals. As a consequence, they also contain very high levels of iodine.

Raw courgette salad,
by Salvatore Romano

Insalata di zucchine

large pale green courgettes
sea salt
juice of 1 lemon
a couple of mint leaves
extra virgin olive oil

The pale green courgettes used by Salvatore for this dish are known in Italian as *Bianca di Trieste*. The Sicilian pale variety, on the other hand, are called *Lungo Bianco di Palermo*. They are almost white inside. Outside Sicily, pale varieties of courgette can be found in Turkish or Greek grocers.

Cut the courgettes into wafer-thin slices. Transfer to a bowl, season with plenty of salt and drizzle with lemon juice, then mix everything gently with your hands. Leave to stand for about 10 minutes. Meanwhile, chop the mint leaves into strips.

Arrange the courgette slices in an overlapping pattern on a serving plate. Scatter over the strips of mint, drizzle with a dash of olive oil and serve immediately.

Catanian tomato salad,
by Salvatore Romano

*Insalata di pomodori
alla Catanese*

plum or cherry tomatoes
red onion, ideally from
    Tropea, sliced into rings
sea salt and freshly ground
    black pepper
ricotta salata, or pecorino
    cheese
extra virgin olive oil

For Salvatore, this recipe is the embodiment of mild summer evenings, preferably spent socializing with friends, getting together, and just enjoying life. The recipe doesn't need much, just some very ripe tomatoes, sweet red onions, some grated *ricotta salata*, and the finest olive oil.

Remove the stalks from the tomatoes and discard. Halve them, then divide between 2 plates.

Scatter the onion rings over the tomatoes. Season with black pepper and grate over some *ricotta salata* (instead of salt).

If you are using pecorino instead, you may also need to sprinkle the salad with a bit of salt to ensure it is adequately seasoned.

Drizzle with olive oil to serve.

LA MONTAGNA

Mount Etna is always in the same place as yesterday, yet always up to something new. Early morning offers a first glimpse: what will today hold? Sometimes it smokes and is good-natured enough to blow out really big smoke rings. Sometimes there's coughing and spluttering. This can be so loud it rattles the doors and windows. The coughing is black and covers everything. Sometimes the mountain sighs and we hear heavy, rasping breathing, as if sickness has taken hold of it. And sometimes things get so hot there is an inevitable explosion, with burning fragments spiralling into the air in a form of artistic display. We love every aspect of this mountain. But one day it will abandon us and head into the ocean. Forever.

Etna, as it is known in Italian, is referred to in Sicilian dialect as *a muntagna* (the mountain) or *u mungibeddu*. The Arabs called Etna *Jabal al-burkān*. Later, she was renamed Mons Gibel, which literally translates as "mountain mountain", as *mons* is Latin for mountain and *jebel* is the same word in Arabic. Sicilians turned this into *mungibeddu*. And *beddu* also means beautiful in Sicilian. Etna lies in the east of Sicily, roughly 30 km (19 miles) from Catania, and is the most active – and highest – volcano in Europe. At the moment the mountain is around 3,330 m (11,000 ft) high. In June 2013 Etna was declared a world heritage site by UNESCO. There are 48 such sites throughout Italy, with Sicily alone boasting six of them.

But Etna is not just a UNESCO site, it is also a paradise for biodiversity, with a magical atmosphere that is impossible to resist. You will find melting snowflakes among the sharp lava rocks. Dense woodland alternates with desert areas packed with volcanic rocks, which are covered in snow in winter. Oak and chestnut forests are joined by beech and birch trees, then there are vineyards, olive groves, orchards, and hazelnut trees, not to mention pistachio groves in the west. The volcanic deposits make the land around Etna extremely fertile, so it is ideal for all kinds of farming. Everything that grows here is of very high quality.

And there is quite an array of produce grown around Etna: it is known for its hazelnuts, walnuts, prickly pears, strawberries from Maletto, pistachios from Bronte, cherries, peaches (*pesca tabacchiera*), small aromatic yellow apples (*cola, gelato,* and *cola-gelato*), and autumn pears such as *ucciardona* and *spinella*, which are ideal varieties for cooking.

This volcanic region is also home to an incredible number of animals, such as porcupines, wild cats, pine martens, foxes, rabbits, and hares, not to mention smaller creatures such as weasels, hedgehogs, and countless species of bat. There are lots of birds as well, especially birds of prey: sparrowhawks, buzzards, kestrels, peregrine falcons, golden eagles, and nocturnal birds such as barn owls and brown owls. At higher levels you will also find partridges and wheatears. Scurrying around on the ground are various kinds of snakes, spiders, and lizards, while the air hums with a variety of insects: butterflies, crickets, grasshoppers, cicadas, and bees. Every single one of these is a vital contributor to the healthy ecosystem of the mountain.

The *Gatto selvatico dell'Etna* is a wild, striped species of cat from the Etna region. And the *Argentata dell'Etna* is another lovely animal: a very special species of goat with long hair, which gets its name from the grey-white-silver hues in its luxurious coat (see p164). These goats look as though they are constantly laughing and have a worldly wise expression.

Local cheeses are produced from their milk, which is particularly rich in protein. One of these cheesemakers is Giuseppe Camuglia, a young man from Castiglione di Sicilia, who works with his father Salvatore in the area close to the wonderful valley landscape around the Alcantara river, making traditional Sicilian cheeses at their dairy Azienda Alcantara. He produces a huge variety of cheeses, including Caprino dei Nebrodi, a mature cheese made from unpasteurised goat's milk. Giuseppe makes this cheese using milk from the Argentata goats and also the black goats *Capra nere dei Nebrodi*. He gets his milk from Nunzio Caruso, who breeds all these wonderful species of goat at the Azienda Acquavena, located in the remote mountain landscape around Bronte.

-lightly baked ricotta-
-ricotta al forno da tavola-

-aged, salted ricotta-
-ricotta salata-

-fresh ricotta-
-ricotta fresca-

-baked ricotta-
-ricotta al forna da grattugia-

Serves 4
Prep 50 mins

Prickly pear skins coated in breadcrumbs

Bucce di fichi d'India a cotoletta

8 prickly pears
sea salt and freshly ground
  black pepper
2 large eggs
160–200g (5³/₄–7oz) fine
  dried breadcrumbs, or
  mollica secca (see p30),
  plus extra if needed
olive oil that can be heated
  to a high temperature,
  or neutral flavoured oil,
  for deep-frying
chilli flakes (optional)

This recipe harks back to times of great poverty on the island and demonstrates the ingenious survival strategies devised by the Sicilian people. The prickly but cheerful-looking *Opuntia ficus-indica* was a plant cultivated by the Aztecs. Every single part of it is edible. The green shoots were not just used as animal fodder, they would have been cooked along with the fruit and its skin. The prickly pear, or *ficho d'India*, is a miraculous fruit that is also extremely healthy, and it propagates very quickly. It is increasingly attracting the attention of both health experts and food lovers.

Experienced Sicilians rarely wear gloves when handling prickly pears, but sturdy gloves are advisable for the rest of us, given the spikes.

Place the prickly pears in cold water for about 10 minutes, then strip or brush off the spikes under running water. Peel each fruit as shown on the left: trim the ends at top and bottom, and discard, then slice the skin lengthways down the middle and fold it to the sides. Remove the interior and reserve.

Blanch the skins for about 5 minutes in generously salted, boiling water. Leave to drain, then dab dry.

In a dish, beat the eggs with salt and pepper. Tip the breadcrumbs into a second dish. Dip the prickly pear skins first into the egg and then the crumbs.

Fill a high-sided pan one-third full with oil and heat this to at least 170°C (340°F) but no higher than 180°C (350°F). Test the temperature by holding a wooden skewer in the oil: you should barely see any little bubbles forming around it. Fry the crumbed skins in batches.

Once they are ready, scoop the skins out using a slotted spoon and leave to drain on kitchen paper. Season with salt and pepper or scatter with chilli flakes (if using) while they are hot, and serve alongside the flesh of the pears.

Orange salad with pecorino and black olives

Insalata di arance con pecorino e olive nere

4 oranges, ideally a mix of
   blood oranges and regular
   oranges
1 large red onion, finely
   sliced into rings
40g (1¼oz) pecorino cheese,
   cut into small, fine slices
100g (3½oz) black olives,
   pitted

For the dressing
1 small mandarin or
   clementine
80ml (2¾oz) extra virgin
   olive oil
sea salt and freshly
   ground black pepper
   or chilli flakes
handful of oregano leaves

This salad is particularly good as a side dish with fried fish, such as Fried Anchovies with Mint (see p63). You can vary it by using other citrus fruits and also serve it with pickled anchovies, if you like.

Peel the oranges, making sure you completely remove the white pith. Slice them into thin rounds, flicking out and discarding any seeds, and put them in a serving dish.

Add the onion rings, pecorino, and olives and gently mix with the orange slices, using your hands.

To make the dressing, squeeze the mandarin or clementine and mix the juice with the oil. Season with salt and pepper or chilli flakes, add the oregano, and mix thoroughly.

Pour the dressing over the orange salad and leave to infuse for a few minutes before serving.

Potato salad with capers, tuna, and olive crumble

Insalata di patate con capperi, tonno, e crumble di olive

For the salad

800g (1³/₄lb) waxy potatoes, cooked and peeled

1 fennel bulb, very finely sliced

300g (10oz) best-quality bluefin tuna, from a jar

200g (7oz) red grapes, halved

100g (3¹/₂oz) large capers

4 sun-dried tomatoes in oil, roughly chopped

1 red onion, finely sliced into rings

handful of mint leaves, roughly torn

handful of basil leaves, roughly torn

1 small red chilli, finely sliced into rings

1 tsp dried marjoram

3 tbsp red wine vinegar, plus extra to taste

80ml (2³/₄fl oz) olive oil, plus extra to taste

sea salt

For the crumble

15g (¹/₂oz) fresh breadcrumbs, or *mollica fresca* (see p30)

1 tbsp sesame seeds

50g (1³/₄oz) black olives, pitted

On the island of Salina, in addition to *pani cunsatu* (see p129), there is another highly acclaimed speciality: potatoes with large capers. It couldn't be simpler! The island cuisine is down-to-earth and pared back to the basics, and if you are lucky enough to get your hands on some of the excellent large capers from Salina or Pantelleria, you should enjoy them just with some potatoes and dressing, in as simple a form as possible. If you are not so fortunate, you can add a couple more ingredients and embellish things a bit, as in this salad recipe.

Chop the potatoes, mix them with all the other salad ingredients in a large bowl, season with salt and leave to infuse for a few minutes.

Meanwhile, toast the breadcrumbs and sesame seeds in a dry frying pan. Leave to cool, then chop with the olives to a rough crumble consistency.

Season the salad to taste with more red wine vinegar or olive oil and adjust the salt. Serve on 4 plates, scattered with the olive crumble.

Braised broccoli

Broccoli affogati

900g (2lb) broccoli
extra virgin olive oil
6 spring onions with a large
  bulb, white parts only,
  finely chopped
3–4 sun-dried tomatoes in
  oil, finely chopped
3–4 anchovy fillets in oil
handful of black olives
chilli flakes
sea salt
90–100ml (3–3½fl oz) dry
  red wine
4 tbsp white wine vinegar
60g (2oz) pecorino cheese,
  finely chopped

Split the broccoli into little florets. Peel a generous layer from the tough stalk and chop its interior into little pieces.

Gently heat some olive oil in a wide, shallow pan. Add the broccoli, spring onions, tomatoes, anchovies, olives, chilli flakes, and some salt. Cover and steam over a medium heat, stirring occasionally as it cooks.

Once the broccoli is partially cooked, uncover, deglaze the pan with the wine and vinegar, increase the heat, and continue cooking until nearly all the liquid has evaporated. About 5 minutes before the end of cooking time, stir in the pecorino. Serve.

This broccoli has an even more intense flavour when cold, so it makes an ideal salad. It is great with the Aubergine Rissoles with Scamorza and Mint served on a Sicilian burger bun (see p125).

Aubergine rissoles with scamorza and mint

Polpette di melanzane con scamorza e menta

1 aubergine (roughly
  300g/10oz)
extra virgin olive oil
1 garlic clove
90g (3¼oz) scamorza cheese,
  finely chopped
30g (1oz) fresh breadcrumbs,
  or *mollica fresca* (see p30)
2 tbsp shredded mint leaves
1 tbsp finely grated
  pecorino cheese
1 tbsp ricotta
1 large egg, lightly beaten
sea salt
chilli flakes

Peel the skin off the aubergine in long strips to create a striped effect, then halve and finely chop. Heat some olive oil in a pan and sauté the aubergine. Transfer onto kitchen paper to absorb some of the oil and leave to cool until lukewarm.

Purée the aubergine with the garlic and scamorza in a food processor. Combine this purée with all the other ingredients in a bowl until you have a fairly firm mixture. Season with salt and chilli flakes. Transfer the bowl to the refrigerator to chill for 30 minutes.

Heat plenty of olive oil in a pan, and use your hands to shape 6 flat rissoles from the mixture. Fry these in the hot oil until brown on all sides. Drain on kitchen paper and serve immediately.

These make wonderful veggie burgers (see p125). Minted Sweet-sour Squash (photo top left) is another great side; (see p111), while Sweet Pickled Peppers (photo bottom right) can be combined with tuna to create a wonderful main course (see p67).

Dolci

LA MANDORLA

In 1872, in his compendium on the almond (*Manuale della coltivazione del mandorlo in Sicilia*), botanist Giuseppe Bianca listed 752 varieties of almond found in Sicily. The most common — *Fascionello*, *Pizzuta d'Avola*, and *Romana* — are predominantly cultivated in the south-eastern province of Syracuse.

To find out more about these three varieties of almond, I visited Concetto Scardaci, a 37-year-old agricultural scientist and almond producer who runs the family business with his wife Valentina on the slopes of Monte Finocchito. He is passionate about his farm, Azienda Agricola Scardaci, where he mainly grows almonds, lemons (*limone di Siracusa* IGP), and carob trees (*carrube*). Like his grandfather before him, who was also called Concetto, he rears sheep too.

Concetto picks me up from Noto in his Jeep, which bears the marks of hard agricultural labour. We lurch with a jolt into a side road. A sign bearing the name Concetto is fixed to a large, stout tree and I see the first glimpses of almond trees dotted here and there. "See this almond grove? It's like an entire population," he says. 'You have two-year old plants, 30-year-olds, and 60-year-olds.

Just like people on a *piazza*. You'll find other species here too, such as olive trees, just as you might find a person from another country in the town square. Nowadays, this kind of arrangement is rare. Here a *Fascionello*, there a *Pizzuta* and a bit further on a *Romana*, all mixed up together. Admittedly it makes harvesting a bit harder work, but the compensation is that you get this stunning view throughout the year," says Concetto enthusiastically of his orchard. He explains his devotion to this approach: "They're not standing there like soldiers in rank and file, all the same age, all the same variety, all compelled to be productive. If my plants are tired, they can simply be unproductive and are allowed to rest. But when they are inclined to produce, they do exactly that, and the quality is absolutely outstanding! Now I'll let you try an almond. You'll declare: 'that is an incredible almond!'"

This year's harvest has been excellent. The nuts here are collected from August until late September, still using the laborious manual approach where the trees are struck with very long canes. After harvesting, the almonds are removed from their green shells and laid out to dry in the sun. Concetto produces all three kinds of almonds, but the *Romana* is his favourite, and the one he chooses to distribute himself in his own packaging. The other two varieties are sold on directly to distributors, still in their brown shells.

"If you remove an almond from its shell today and don't eat it for another two months, during that time the nut absorbs flavours and scents from its surroundings.

Sicilia   California

Depending on the environment and storage, this may be suboptimal. You only get that original flavour if you crack them open to eat straight away," says Concetto. So should you always buy almonds in their shells? "Ideally yes, but over time the shell becomes so hard that it can't be removed with standard domestic tools. You will need a hard stone and a really heavy-duty mallet."

The *Romana* bears the name of a family from the town of Avola, which was supposedly involved in the nut variety's cultivation and dissemination. This is the almond that bears the finest fruit when it comes to taste, appearance, and texture. It is the nut of choice for Sicilian *pasticcerie* and – thanks to its slightly bitter flavour – it is also ideal for savoury dishes. This is also the almond that was included in the Slow Food Ark of Taste around 20 years ago (under its alternative name, *Mandorla di Noto*, see right). This ancient, resistant almond has just one flaw: the shape of its kernel. Because the shell nearly always contains two almonds, they are irregular in shape. The rather crumpled kernels cannot be used for sugared almonds – or *confetti*,

as they are known here – which are popular for festivities. As a result, this variety has been rather neglected – maybe even discriminated against – over recent years. However, lately it has been in demand again, because it has such an excellent flavour. The *Pizzuta*, meanwhile, is considered the queen of almonds largely thanks to its elegant shape. Consequently, this is the almond of choice for making *confetti*. The *Fascionello* lies somewhere between the two. Its shape is as regular and appealing as the *Pizzuta*, so it is also used for *confetti*, and it has a robust flavour, similar to that of the *Romana*.

Every almond tree is derived from the bitter almond (*Prunus dulcis* var. *amara*). These seeds are sown in seedbeds for their first year and that's where they stay, safe and sound for the whole seasonal cycle. After that time, when they have learned to survive, the little bitter almond shoots are transferred to an orchard to join the other trees. After two years, once they have become well-established, the desired variety of almond – whether *Romana*, *Pizzuta*, or *Fascionello* – is grafted onto the tree.

Pizzuta   Fascionello   Romana

In addition to the three best-known varieties of almond, Concetto also grows a large number of almost unknown, ancient species for himself. For instance, *Chiricupara* (which has a kernel similar to an apricot, except slightly larger), *Scacciunara* (a very flat almond), *Miuzza* (a very small nut), *Cuore* (a rare, heart-shaped variety), and *Rappitieddo* (which forms very small kernels that develop closely packed together). These varieties are still in danger of being lost – both the names and the plants – unless the younger generation can somehow keep them alive.

There is a certain amount of confusion between the *Mandorla di Noto* and the *Mandorla d'Avola*. Originally, just a single variety was designated as *Mandorla d'Avola*, namely the highly regarded *Pizzuta*, also known as *Pizzuta d'Avola*. In the past, this almond was marketed by traders from the town of Avola as being the best for *confetti* (unfortunately, almonds on Sicily have been routinely judged solely in terms of their suitability for *confetti*). Even though most of the almonds were grown in Noto and the surrounding area, as they still are today, they

were sold as *Mandorla Pizzuta d'Avola*. So every almond variety in Avola was called a *Mandorla d'Avola*. Hence the confusion. It means *Mandorla d'Avola* also refers to the *Romana* variety, even though this has had Slow Food protected status as *La Mandorla di Noto* for 20 years.

The added "*Noto*" designation only came about because, at the time when Slow Food first included the almond in its Ark, 70 per cent of almond producers came from Noto and its surroundings. Before this, almonds from the region were simply referred to as *La Corrente d'Avola*, and included any number of different varieties. To put it simply: both *Mandorla di Noto* and *Mandorla d'Avola* ultimately refer to the same three varieties of almond.

Serves 4
Prep 15 mins, plus
   cooling time

Almond blancmange

Biancomangiare

80g (2³/₄oz) cornflour
1 litre (1³/₄ pints)
   unsweetened almond milk
   (for home-made, see p220)
120–140g (4¹/₄–5oz) caster
   sugar or honey
zest of 1 organic lemon,
   without the white pith,
   chopped into pieces
400g (14oz) cow's milk
   ricotta (optional)
ground cinnamon, or chopped
   pistachios and jasmine
   flowers, to garnish

This recipe is a variant on my basic blancmange. I definitely prefer to use cornflour rather than plain flour. If desired, I sometimes stir some melted chocolate into the mixture instead of ricotta, or maybe fold in some pistachio cream made using pistachios from Bronte. If the blancmange is made without ricotta, the resulting pudding can be turned out of a mould (see photos) and decorated with edible flowers such as jasmine and chopped pistachios.

In a small bowl, stir the cornflour into about 200ml (7fl oz) of the almond milk and mix well.

In a saucepan, combine the remaining almond milk with the sugar and lemon zest, then stir in the cornflour mixture. Place over a medium heat and cook, stirring constantly with a whisk until it comes to the boil. Cook for a few minutes, continuing to stir until the mixture thickens.

Remove the pan from the heat and leave to cool until lukewarm.

Strain the mixture to remove the lemon zest, then stir in the ricotta, if using. Divide the creamy mixture between 4 dessert glasses or small bowls and chill for at least 2 hours.

Dust with ground cinnamon to serve.

CORRADO

Someone who has made a significant contribution
to the reappraisal of the *Romana* almond is Corrado
Assenza, the world-famous Sicilian *pasticciere* who
owns Caffè Sicilia in Noto. In his view, the *Romana*
is the best (see p180 for more on Sicilian almonds).

So my next stop is with Corrado in Noto, where I will get
to know this nut a bit better. My order is initially all-white:
granita alla mandorla and *biancomangiare*. Then Corrado
serves me something black, a *gelato al gelso nero* (black
mulberry gelato), to offer my stomach a contrast.
Incidentally, he later tells me that *biancomangiare* was his
mother's favourite dessert. The *Romana* is his preferred
almond for making granita, mousse, blancmange,
and almond milk, because its fat content offers a more
intense taste experience when compared to the other two
common varieties of almond (*Pizzuta* and *Fascionello*).

Over 33 years ago, when Caffè Sicilia still belonged to his
aunt, this simple yet sophisticated dessert wasn't even on
the menu here. The wonderful thing about his version is
that you taste the almonds rather than the cornflour.
There's no trick to this, it's all down to skill, says Corrado:
finding the right producer for your cornflour and also
using the correct quantity. You can't just mix any old
almond milk with any old cornflour.

Corrado is an incredibly polite and fairly taciturn man. In
his free time – if he gets any – he loves to read. He barely
watches any television, but he did appear in the successful
Netflix series *Chef's Table*. His first choice of career wasn't
even to become a *pasticciere*. His aunt phoned him when
he was studying entomology in Bologna and presented
him with a choice: "Either you come back to Sicily and
take over the café, or the café will have to close."
He abandoned his dream of becoming a bee expert and,
instead, became one of the most famous *pasticcieri*
on the island.

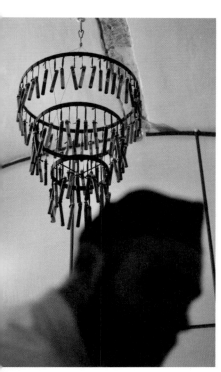

Pistachio pastry

Paste di pistacchio

120g (4¼oz) icing sugar, plus
  extra for dusting
340g (11½oz) pistachios,
  ideally from Bronte,
  140g (5oz) finely ground in
  a mortar and pestle
1 medium egg white
60g (2oz) fine "00" grade
  durum wheat semolina flour
finely grated zest of
  ¼ organic lemon
5–7 drops of mandarin oil
5–7 drops of bitter almond oil

Sicilian pistachio production is located in Bronte, close to Mount Etna. The volcano supplies the soil with an abundance of nutrients (for more details, see p164); that is the benefit of having a volcano as your immediate neighbour. The drawback is that Bronte has already been destroyed three times by cascading lava flows! However, this pistachio-growing town with its 19,000 residents, 50km (31 miles) north-west of Catania, accepts its fate. One reason why pistachios (which are also referred to as "green gold") are so expensive is because they can only be harvested every two years, in August, by hand. Understandably, this is a cause for celebration. In late September every year, Bronte holds the festival of the pistachio, *La sagra del pistacchio.*

Combine all the ingredients except the whole pistachios and knead until you have a firm dough. Leave to rest in the refrigerator for 1 hour.

Preheat the oven to 180°C (350°F/ Gas 4). Line a baking tray with baking parchment. Put the whole pistachios on a plate.

Dust a work surface generously with icing sugar and create 2 rolls (roughly 2.5cm/1in in diameter) from the dough. Cut these into roughly 6cm- (2½in-) long pieces and gently press one long side of each into the whole pistachios. Round off the ends of each pastry slightly, arrange them spaced out on the prepared tray and bake in the centre of the oven for 10 minutes.

Remove from the oven and use all your willpower to resist eating them until they have cooled down!

MARIA

On a 750 metre- (820 yard-) high mountain, in the very far west of the island, is perched a little medieval town that was originally inhabited by the Elymians before the eighth century BCE (see p10). It was known as Eryx. It did not acquire its current name, Erice, until 1934.

The town boasts 60 churches, the Castle of Venus (*Castello di Venere*), and ancient town walls with three imposing gates. It has countless twisting, cobblestoned alleyways and offers magnificent panoramic views (depending on the visibility) over the west coast and as far as the Aegadian island archipelago. It is also home to its very own queen.

I am referring to Maria Grammatico, in her capacity as the uncrowned queen of Sicilian convent desserts. She gained renown thanks to the book, *Bitter Almonds*, published in 1994. It is a memoir of her girlhood in a convent, with recipes from the nuns, written by the American Mary Taylor Simeti. Mary met Maria quite by chance on Sicily and, through the book's publication, Maria became a Sicilian celebrity.

Maria Grammatico's father died when she was eleven years old, leaving behind a destitute and newly pregnant wife, who already had five other children. Her mother was faced with two options for the family: either her daughters would have to go into domestic service, or they could enter a convent. Maria and her younger sister Angela were sent to the San Carlo convent in Erice. An uncle advised her mother to get the children there before Christmas, so they would have something to eat during the festive season.

San Carlo was once a cloistered convent, but it was expropriated by Mussolini during the Second World War and transformed into a secular institution. Since then it has been under the administration of the municipal social services office, although life in the convent continued as usual. Maria stayed at the convent from 1952 to 1962 and there, hidden away from the world, she learned the art of making the convent's delicious sweets. Or, to be more accurate, Maria stole this expertise from the convent, because the nuns guarded their baking secrets warily. They were both suspicious and stingy. But little Maria watched their baking carefully and noted everything in her head.

Apart from alms and donations, the production of *dolci* was the only way for nuns to make money. And it ensured the livelihood of everyone who lived in the convent. All 18 children there were needed to help the 15 nuns with this strenuous physical work, even on holy Sundays.

At baking time, the children would have to get up in the cold at 1am to heat up the oven before the nuns arrived around 4am. From 6am, little delicacies such as *mostaccioli* and *biscotti* would be baked. Needless to say, none of the baked goods were wasted on the children, or at least only if they were burned and inedible, so effectively unsellable. Not surprisingly, then, it wasn't unheard of for the junior baking assistants to accidentally-on-purpose lose track of the baking times...

Maria, who is now 79, recalls: "Food was scarce and the nuns were always more concerned with their own livelihoods than with the welfare of the children. Anyone who had money could buy themselves extra food." But Maria and her sister Angela were among those children who had no money at all. There are lots of painful little episodes that have remained etched in Maria's memory. For instance, the time the two girls watched the nuns gleefully enjoying oranges and mandarins. Angela

meekly approached one of the nuns and politely asked if she might have a piece of orange, but the nun gave her nothing.

Maria subsequently left the convent and, in June 1964, after suffering an emotional breakdown, she decided to open up a little shop. Even then, the nuns showed no inclination to give her any baking tins, or even to lend her a few items. She started with no money and just 3kg (6½lb) of almonds. And she had to make her own baking tins from plaster.

Ever since then, Maria has reflected a great deal on Christian values, such as charity. She still believes in God, but she no longer has faith in the church.

In 1975, Maria also opened her *pasticceria* in Via Vittorio Emanuele and, later still, the Pasticceria del Vechio Convento, which is now run by her sister. For decades her

life has followed the same annual rhythms, just like life back in the convent: Christmas hearts in December, *cannoli* for carnival season, Easter lambs for Easter.

After her success, Maria wanted to reintroduce the tradition that lived on through her work to the place where she had learned her skills: the Convento San Carlo. The convent was closed in 1969, so she asked the municipality for a small site in the old walls where she would be able to continue this tradition. But they gave her nothing.

Maria's tale is the age-old story of so many Sicilians, somehow finding the most wonderful way to remain strong in the face of virtually intolerable circumstances. *Mandorle amare* translates as "bitter almonds". But the word *amare* in Italian also means "love".

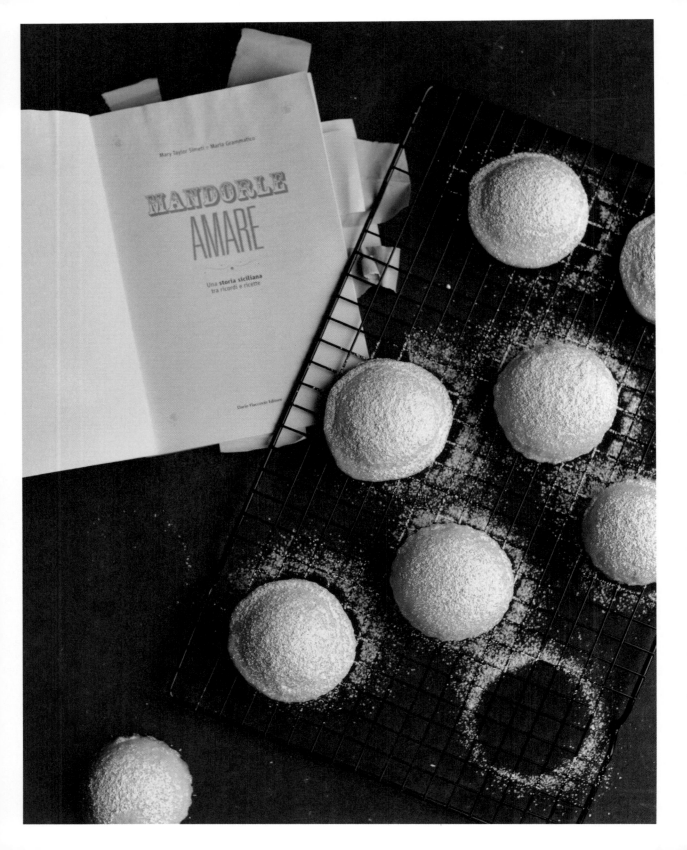

Cream-filled shortcrust pastries – inspired by Maria Grammatico's recipe

Genovesi

For the pastry
125g (4¹/₂oz) "00" pasta
    flour, plus extra to dust
125g (4¹/₂oz) fine durum
    wheat semolina flour
pinch of sea salt
70g (2¹/₄oz) caster sugar
2 large egg yolks
100g (3¹/₂oz) chilled
    unsalted butter, cubed
icing sugar, to dust

For the crème pâtissière
1 large egg yolk
30g (1oz) caster sugar
sea salt
20g (³/₄oz) cornflour
250ml (9fl oz) whole milk
zest of ¹/₄ organic lemon

You just *have* to order these at Maria Grammatico's *pasticceria*. The origin of the name is a mystery to Maria: "Maybe I was in love with someone from Genoa once? I'm not sure myself any more!" Maria's *genovesi* are reminiscent of the *Minni di virgini* found in Palermo, but those are slightly more domed and have added candied fruits and little chunks of chocolate. Maria doesn't make them following the original recipe from Sor Angelica in San Carlo, whose speciality this dish was, for the simple reason that she was never given it!

For the pastry, put the flour and semolina in a food processor with the salt, sugar, egg yolks, butter, and 4 tbsp water and process to combine. Shape into a ball, wrap in cling film, and refrigerate for 1 hour.

Meanwhile, for the crème pâtissière, use a balloon whisk or electric hand whisk to beat the egg yolk with the sugar and a pinch of salt until foamy. Stir the cornflour into roughly 50ml (1³/₄fl oz) of the milk, then combine this with the remaining milk in a saucepan. Stir the milk mixture into the egg yolk mixture, then place over a medium heat, stirring constantly with a whisk, until the custard thickens. Pour it into a bowl and fold in the lemon zest. Put cling film directly on the surface to prevent a skin from forming and leave to cool completely.

Preheat the oven to 220°C (425°F/ Gas 7). Line a baking tray with baking parchment.

Roll out the pastry on a lightly floured work surface until 4mm (¹/₄in) thick, then stamp out circles about 10cm (4in) in diameter. Spoon 1–1½ tbsp crème pâtissière into the centre of each pastry round. Place a second pastry round on top and press the edges down firmly with your fingers.

Transfer the *genovesi* to the prepared tray. Bake in the centre of the oven for 12–15 minutes until they begin to colour slightly.

Remove from the oven, transfer to a wire rack, and sift over icing sugar while they are still hot. *Genovesi* are best enjoyed lukewarm.

Serves 2
Prep 25 mins, plus
   freezing time

Coffee ice-cream sundae with hot chocolate sauce

Caldofreddo

120g (4¼oz) whipping cream,
   plus 2 tbsp extra
300ml (½ pint) coffee ice
   cream (shop-bought, or
   follow the recipe below)
4 sponge fingers or 70g
   (2¼oz) sponge (see p199)
2 tbsp Marsala or rum
100g (3½oz) dark chocolate
2 tsp chopped hazelnuts

At Gelateria Liparoti, run by Maurizio Liparoti from Trapani, I sample unusual ice creams such as liquorice (*liquirizia* DOP) and carob seed (*carruba*). He also makes *caldofreddo*, for which the province of Trapani is famous. This is a classic home-made sundae served in Trapani's ice-cream parlours and was first created back in 1950 in San Vito Lo Capo. It is traditionally served in a little glazed terracotta bowl known as a *lemmo*.

Whip the cream until stiff and put it in the freezer until solid.

Scoop coffee ice cream into 2 bowls (ideally *lemmi*), and make a hollow in each. Crumble in the sponge fingers, soak with Marsala, and smooth the ice cream back over. Add a scoop of frozen cream to each and return to the freezer for at least 5 minutes.

Meanwhile, melt the chocolate with 2 tbsp cream over a bain-marie and set aside to keep warm. The chocolate sauce must not be allowed to simmer!

Fetch the bowls of ice cream from the freezer, pour over the hot chocolate sauce, scatter with hazelnuts, and serve immediately.

Serves 2
Prep 30 mins, plus
   freezing time

Coffee ice cream

Gelato al caffè

75ml (2½fl oz) whole milk
75ml (2½fl oz) espresso,
   freshly made
150g (5½oz) whipping cream
½ tsp instant coffee
seeds from 1 vanilla pod
4 medium egg yolks
30g (1oz) sugar

Stir the milk, espresso, cream, instant coffee, and vanilla in a saucepan, then briefly bring to the boil. Remove from the heat and cool slightly.

In a steel bowl over a bain-marie at about 80°C (175°F), whisk the egg yolks and sugar, then pour in the coffee mixture in a thin stream, stirring constantly until it thickens. Put the bowl into a bowl of ice cubes and stir until the cream cools down.

Transfer to an ice-cream maker and churn according to the manufacturer's instructions. Freeze until serving.

Serves 4
Prep 50 mins, plus baking
and cooling time

Layered dessert with crème pâtissière and Marsala

Testa di Turco

For the sponge
2 medium eggs, separated
80g (2³/₄oz) caster sugar
1 tsp finely grated zest of
   1 organic lemon
¹/₄ tsp vanilla bean paste
pinch of fine sea salt
50g (1³/₄oz) "00" pasta flour
8g (¹/₄oz) baking powder
40g (1¹/₄oz) cornflour

For the crème pâtissière
1 litre (1³/₄ pints) whole
   milk
140g (5oz) caster sugar
pared zest from 1 small
   organic lemon, without
   the white pith
80g (2³/₄oz) cornflour

For finishing the dessert
40g (1¹/₄oz) caster sugar
4 tbsp sweet Marsala
   (ideally *semisecco*)
1–2 heaped tsp ground
   cinnamon
colourful sprinkles

For me, this dessert evokes the ancient aromas of Sicily, and, for many Sicilians, it is the taste of childhood. It can also be made with *savoiardi* (Sicilian sponge fingers) instead of home-made sponge, and goes by different names in different homes. *Testa di Turco* literally means "the head of the Turk", and harks back to the ancient battles to conquer Sicily. The recipe originates in Castelbuono, where fried pastry is used instead of sponge as a special carnival dish.

Preheat the oven to 180°C (350°F/ Gas 4). Line a rectangular baking dish (roughly 25×19cm / 10 x 7½in) with baking parchment.

Beat the egg yolks with 50g (1¾oz) of the sugar, the lemon zest, and vanilla until creamy. Whisk the egg whites with 2 tbsp cold water and the salt until stiff. Gradually whisk in the remaining sugar until well combined.

Gently but thoroughly fold the stiff egg whites into the egg yolk mixture. Combine the flour, baking powder, and cornflour, sift them over the egg mixture and fold in carefully. Transfer to the baking dish and bake for 25–30 minutes. Allow to cool, then slice the sponge in half horizontally.

To make the crème pâtissière, mix 800ml (1 pint 7fl oz) of the milk with the sugar and pared lemon zest in a saucepan. Stir the remaining milk into the cornflour in a bowl, mixing well,

then stir this into the milk and lemon mixture. Bring to the boil, stirring constantly with a balloon whisk, then continue to stir for a few minutes over a medium heat until it thickens. Remove from the heat and leave to cool slightly. Discard the lemon zest.

To finish, mix 160ml (5½fl oz) water with the sugar in a small saucepan, simmer it down slightly, then leave to cool. Stir in the Marsala.

In the dish in which you baked the sponge, drizzle the first sponge layer with half the Marsala mixture. Spread half the crème pâtissière on top and dust with half the cinnamon. Repeat the layers.

Chill the dessert for at least 1 hour. Sprinkle with colourful sugar balls shortly before serving.

Serves 8
Prep 1 hr 50 mins, plus
    cooling time

Sicilian cassata torte

Cassata al forno

For the ricotta cream
600g (1lb 5oz) ricotta
1 tsp vanilla bean paste
120g (4¹/₄oz) caster sugar
pinch of fine sea salt
zest of 1 small organic orange
zest of 1 small organic lemon
60g (2oz) dark chocolate chips
1¹/₂ tbsp chopped pistachios

For the pastry
200g (7oz) "00" pasta flour,
    plus more to dust
70g (2¹/₄oz) caster sugar
100g (3¹/₂oz) cold unsalted
    butter, chopped, plus extra
    for the tin
1 medium egg yolk
1 generous tbsp sweet Marsala
¹/₂ tsp vanilla bean paste
pinch of fine sea salt
zest of ¹/₂ small organic
    lemon

For the sponge
1 medium egg, separated, plus
    1 medium egg white (from
    the pastry)
pinch of fine sea salt
40g (1¹/₄oz) caster sugar
1 tbsp zest of 1 organic
    orange
15g (¹/₂oz) fine "00" grade
    durum wheat semolina flour
1 level tsp baking powder
10g (¹/₄oz) cornflour
10g (¹/₄oz) cocoa powder
2 tbsp sweet Marsala

icing sugar
ground cinnamon

Cassata used to be reserved for Easter in Sicily, but now it's available all year round. The world-renowned *cassata Siciliana*, that is covered in marzipan, actually evolved from this original version. In the past, it consisted simply of shortcrust pastry with a sweet ricotta filling.

To make the ricotta cream, mix the ricotta with the vanilla, sugar, salt, and zests in a bowl. Place a sieve over another bowl and pour in the creamy mixture. Leave it to drip through the sieve for 2 hours in the refrigerator.

Meanwhile, quickly combine all the ingredients for the pastry, wrap in cling film, and chill for 1 hour.

Preheat the oven to 180°C (350°F/ Gas 4) and line the base of an 18cm (7in) cake tin with baking parchment.

For the sponge, whisk both egg whites with the salt until foamy. Trickle in half the sugar, whisking until the egg whites are firm. Beat the egg yolk with the remaining sugar and the orange zest until foamy. Carefully fold the whisked egg whites into the egg yolk mixture.

Combine the flour with the baking powder, cornflour, and cocoa. Fold this into the egg mixture in small batches.

Spoon into the tin and bake in the centre of the oven for 15–18 minutes. Test it is done by inserting a skewer; it should emerge clean. The sponge will rise to a height of at least 2cm (³/₄in). Leave to cool, then release from the tin. Slice in half horizontally.

Butter another tin 20cm (8in) in diameter, and line the base and sides with baking parchment.

Set aside 120–150g (4¹/₄–5¹/₂oz) pastry for the top of the cake. Roll out the remaining pastry as thinly as possible on a floured work surface. Use this to line the tin. Now place a sponge layer inside and drizzle with 1 tbsp Marsala. Fold the chocolate chips and pistachios into the ricotta cream and spread over the sponge. Cover with the second sponge layer. Drizzle with the remaining Marsala.

Roll out a lid from the remaining shortcrust and prick with a fork, then lay it over the torte and pinch to seal the edges all the way round. Bake in the centre of the oven for 50 minutes. Test it is done by inserting a wooden skewer.

Leave to cool, then dust with icing sugar and cinnamon, in a decorative pattern if desired. This tastes even better the next day!

Strawberry granita

Granita alla fragola

80g (2³/₄oz) sugar, plus extra
    if needed
100ml (3¹/₂fl oz) freshly
    squeezed orange juice
¹/₄ tsp vanilla bean paste
500g (1lb 2oz) ripe
    strawberries
2 tbsp pomegranate liqueur
    or rose liqueur
juice and finely grated
    zest of 1 organic lemon
whipped cream, to serve
    (optional)

The best granita, so it is said, can be found in Catania. Some people make a more specific claim for Noto, while others swear by the superiority of Taormina, to be precise Saretto Bambara's Bam Bar. Traditionally there were only three kinds of granita in Sicily: lemon (*granita al limone*), coffee (*granita al caffè*), and almond (*granita alla mandorla*). Another particular speciality these days is mulberry (*granita con gelsi*), available in both black and white (*gelsi neri, gelsi bianchi*). But strawberry granita has gradually gained in popularity alongside the many other varieties now available. Granita, with or without cream, served with a brioche is the trendiest summer breakfast in Sicily. People are getting creative and there have been some radical innovations: how about a refreshing *granita al limone* in a glass of beer...?

Chill a shallow container ahead of time in the freezer compartment.

Put the sugar, orange juice, and vanilla in a saucepan and bring to the boil. Simmer this down slightly over a medium heat for 3 minutes. Remove from the heat and leave the syrup to cool completely.

Clean the strawberries, chop roughly and put them in a blender with the liqueur, a few splashes of lemon juice, and the lemon zest. Purée.

Mix the strawberry purée with the cooled syrup, then transfer to the pre-frozen container and put this in the freezer for at least 6 hours.

After about 1 hour, stir the mixture with a fork. Repeat this process every hour, to keep the ice crystals nice and small and trap air in the mixture.

After 5 hours, blitz the granita with a hand-held blender to break down the ice crystals. Return it to the freezer for another hour.

Scoop the granita into glasses and serve with whipped cream, if you like, and a brioche bun (for home-made, see p125).

Traditional Sicilian orange cake

Pan d'arancio

For the cake

1 small organic orange
  (around 120g / 4¼oz)
3 medium eggs
seeds from ½ vanilla pod
80g (2¾oz) demerara sugar
50g (1¾oz) caster sugar
1 generous tbsp almond or
  orange liqueur
100g (3½oz) unsalted butter,
  melted and cooled, plus
  extra for greasing
fine durum wheat semolina
  flour, for the tin
100g (3½oz) "00" pasta flour
50g (1¾oz) ground almonds
1 tsp baking powder
pinch of fine sea salt

For the icing and decoration

2 tsp orange juice or liqueur
100g (3½oz) icing sugar, plus
  extra to dust (optional)
finely grated zest of
  1 organic orange
candied orange slices
  (optional)

What an ingenious idea it was from the Sicilians to throw whole citrus fruits into this cake. After all, why bother peeling an orange when it's the skin that has most of the flavour? This cake can also be made with lemons, mandarins, or clementines. And instead of butter, which was not as widely available in Sicily in the past, you can substitute olive oil. The story goes that monks at the Benedictine monastery in Catania invented this cake – while we'll never know for sure, they certainly had a reputation as true food connoisseurs.

Wash the orange in hot water and chop into pieces, but do not peel! Remove any pips. Purée the orange in a food processor.

Use an electric whisk or free-standing mixer to beat the eggs with the vanilla, both types of sugar, and the almond or orange liqueur for about 5 minutes until the mixture is pale and creamy.

Preheat the oven to 180°C (350°F/ Gas 4). Grease a large loaf tin (800–900ml / 1¼–1½ pints in volume) and dust with semolina flour.

Gradually stir the orange purée and butter into the egg mixture. Mix the flour with the ground almonds, baking powder, and salt. Fold the dry ingredients in batches into the egg mixture. Spoon into the tin and bake in the bottom of the oven for 45–50 minutes, until a skewer inserted into the centre emerges clean. Leave to cool, then turn out of the tin.

To make the icing, gradually stir drops of juice or liqueur into the icing sugar until you have a viscous glaze. Pour this over the cooled cake. (If you like, you can dust the cake with icing sugar beforehand.) Sprinkle with orange zest and decorate with candied orange slices, if you like.

For lemon and olive oil cake (*pan di limone*):

Replace the butter with 80ml (2¾fl oz) olive oil, use lemon instead of orange, and limoncello or amaretto instead of orange liqueur.

Watermelon pudding

Gelo di anguria

1 watermelon (1–1.2kg /
    2¼–2¾lb)
1 cinnamon stick
handful of jasmine flowers,
    plus extra to garnish
40g (1¼oz) cornflour
60–80g (2–2¾oz) sugar,
    depending on how sweet
    the melon is
handful of pistachios,
    roughly chopped
handful of dark chocolate,
    chopped

A sun-ripened watermelon, with seeds, is perfect just as it is and requires no further tinkering. Nonetheless, this pudding is worth the effort. Palermo's inhabitants dedicated this dish to Santa Rosalia, their patron saint. At the *Festino di Santa Rosalia* on 15 July, traditional dishes include *pasta con le sarde* (see p29), *babbaluci* (snails cooked with garlic and parsley), and watermelon in every conceivable variation: served simply as it comes, made into pudding as an accompaniment to sweet pies (*crostata*; the recipe here is ideal for that purpose), as watermelon ice cream, or as granita. The fruit belongs to the family of cucurbits (*Cucurbitaceae*) along with cucumbers, and comes originally from Africa, but now it is grown anywhere with nice, warm conditions.

Juice the melon; you will need 500ml (16fl oz) juice for this recipe. Cover and chill the juice overnight with the cinnamon stick and jasmine flowers. The next day, strain the juice.

Stir the cornflour into 100ml (3½fl oz) of the juice, then dissolve this in the remaining juice. Add sugar to taste and cook in a saucepan over a medium heat, stirring constantly, until the juice has thickened to a creamy consistency. Remove from the heat and divide the mixture between 4 moulds, which you have rinsed in cold water immediately beforehand. Chill for at least 5 hours.

Turn the watermelon puddings out onto dessert plates and decorate with pistachios, chocolate, and jasmine flowers to serve.

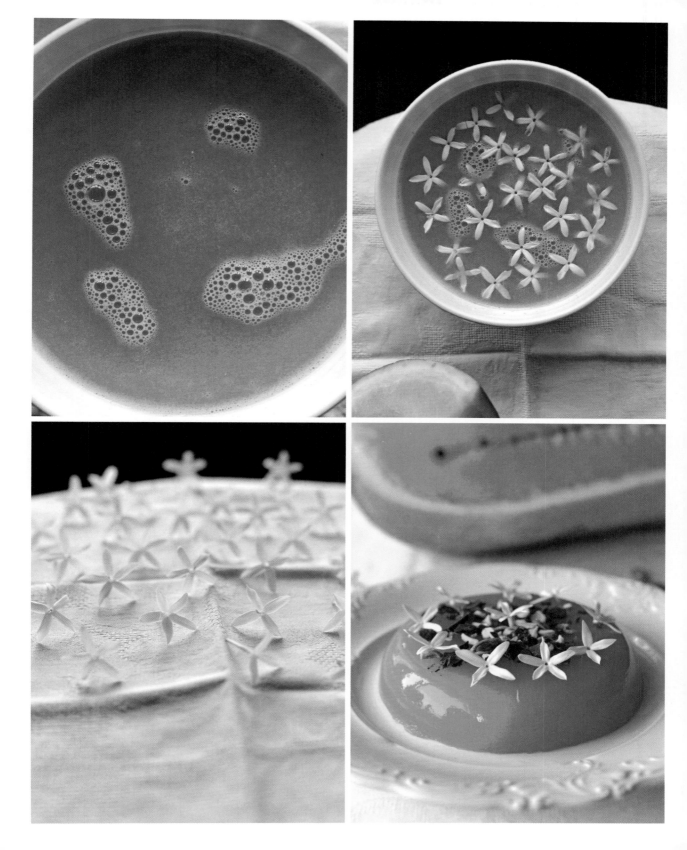

Ricotta and wheat berry cakes

Lucia e Agata

Makes 4
Prep 1½ hrs, plus soaking
and draining time

St Lucia lived in Syracuse, St Agata in Catania, both almost 2,000 years ago. They devoted themselves to the Christian faith and suffered as a consequence. Here I have created a single dessert that combines *cuccìa* (boiled wheat berries in a sweet ricotta cream), which is served in Syracuse for Santa Lucia on 13 December, and *minne di Sant'Agata*, which are small cassata cakes.

For the wheat berry cream

120g (4¼oz) wheat berries
1 large piece each of organic
    orange and organic lemon
    zest, white pith removed
1 bay leaf
pinch of sea salt
250g (9oz) ricotta
35g (1¼oz) caster sugar
20g (¾oz) dark chocolate,
    roughly chopped
generous pinch of finely
    grated zest from 1 organic
    orange and 1 organic lemon
1 tsp ground cinnamon
1 tbsp maraschino liqueur
    (cherry liqueur), plus
    2 tbsp for soaking
15g (½oz) candied lemon
    peel, chopped

For the sponge mixture

1 medium egg
40g (1¼oz) caster sugar,
    plus 2 tbsp for soaking
25g (scant 1oz) fine "00"
    grade durum wheat
    semolina flour
1 tsp baking powder
pinch of fine sea salt
20g (¾oz) cornflour

For the decoration

160g (5¾oz) pistachio paste,
    or marzipan coloured with
    green food colouring
splash of lemon juice
100g (3½oz) icing sugar
4 glacé cherries

Soak the wheat berries in 1 litre (1¾ pints) of water for 12 hours, then drain. Put them in a saucepan with 1 litre (1¾ pints) fresh water and the large pieces of citrus zests, bay leaf, and salt and cook for 1 hour until soft. Drain and leave to cool, discarding the zests and bay leaf.

Mix the ricotta with the sugar, chocolate, finely grated citrus zests, cinnamon, liqueur, candied lemon peel, and wheat berries. Spoon into a sieve over a bowl and leave to drain in the refrigerator for 3 hours.

Preheat the oven to 180°C (350°F/ Gas 4). Line a 20cm (8in) square cake tin with baking parchment.

To make the sponge, beat the egg with the sugar until creamy. Mix the flour, baking powder, salt, and cornflour, sift this over the egg mixture and fold it in.

Transfer to the prepared tin and bake for 15 minutes. Leave to cool on a wire rack, then stamp out 4 circles the same size as the moulds you'll use.

Divide the pistachio paste or marzipan into 4. Roll out each piece between 2 sheets of cling film to create discs 13–14cm (5–5½in) in diameter and 2–3mm (⅛in) thick. These should each be able to line a hemisphere mould with a capacity of about 100ml (3½fl oz). Remove the top layer of cling film. Transfer each disc into one of the moulds with the cling film at the bottom. Fill with wheat berry cream almost to the rim.

Make the mixture for soaking the sponge by heating 4 tbsp water with the 2 tbsp sugar until it has dissolved. Leave to cool, then stir in the 2 tbsp liqueur. Drizzle the mixture over the sponge, position the sponge circles on top of the wheat berry cream, then turn the little cakes out of the moulds. Pull off the cling film and trim off any excess pistachio paste around the edges.

In a bowl, stir sufficient lemon juice into the icing sugar to create a liquid but not excessively runny glaze. Pour over the little cakes to cover completely. Top each with a glacé cherry. Chill for at least 1 hour before serving.

209

Makes 10–12
Preparation time 2 hrs, plus
    cooling time

Cannoli with artichoke cream

Cannoli con crema di carciofi

For the filling

5 artichokes
coarse sea salt
250g (9oz) ricotta, ideally
    sheep's milk ricotta
50–60g (1¾–2oz) icing sugar,
    plus extra for decorating
30g (1oz) candied lemon peel,
    finely chopped
50g (1¾oz) dark chocolate,
    roughly chopped (optional)
¼ tsp vanilla bean paste
pinch of fine sea salt
chopped hazelnuts, for
    decorating

For the pastry tubes

1 small egg
pinch of sea salt
140g (5oz) "00" pasta flour,
    plus extra for dusting
25g (scant 1oz) lard
15g (½oz) icing sugar
2 tbsp Marsala
1 tbsp red wine vinegar
pinch of ground cinnamon
neutral flavoured oil, for
    deep-frying

You can tell whether a *cannolo* was made in Palermo or Catania depending on how it is decorated: in Catania they use chopped pistachios, in Palermo they prefer candied orange zest. The municipality of Ramacca, 45km (28 miles) from Catania, is famous for its purple artichokes (*carciofi violetti di Ramacca*) and here, during their artichoke festival, you will find a truly revolutionary approach to using this vegetable. The *cannolo* in question comes from the Pasticceria Ricca and consists of two pastry tubes: a smaller one, filled with chocolate cream, and a larger one filled with a ricotta and artichoke cream. I have simplified the recipe somewhat.

To make the filling, first discard the tough, outer leaves of the artichokes. Trim about 1.5cm (½in) from the stalks and pare off the hard outer, fibrous section. Put them in a saucepan, cover with water, season lightly with salt, cover, and cook over a low heat for 25–30 minutes. Drain thoroughly, then dab dry.

Scrape the flesh off the artichoke leaves using the back of a knife. Purée the flesh with the artichoke hearts and stalk in a food processor, then press through a fine sieve. Stir in the remaining filling ingredients. Spoon into a sieve over a bowl and leave to drain in the refrigerator for 3 hours.

For the pastry, gently beat the egg with the salt and mix this with the other ingredients until they come together. Shape into a ball, wrap in cling film and refrigerate for 1 hour.

In a pan, heat the oil for frying to 180°C (350°F/Gas 4). Hold a wooden skewer in the oil to test: when little bubbles form on it, the oil is hot enough.

Roll out the pastry as thinly as possible on a floured work surface and divide into 10cm (4in) squares. Place metal tubes to shape the cannoli diagonally on the pastry. Moisten a corner of each square, roll it up loosely around the tube, and press down the corner.

Cook each roll for 3–4 minutes in the hot oil until golden. They should have enough space to turn without touching, so you may have to cook them in batches. Drain on kitchen paper, leave to cool, then carefully pull out the metal tubes.

Spoon the cream into a piping bag and fill the tubes. Sift icing sugar over, scatter nuts on each end, and serve.

Bevande

IL CHIOSCO

Green mandarin and lemon (*mandarino verde e limone*), or "Lemon lemon" (*limone limone*), or even tamarind and lemon (*tamarindo e limone*) — all of these drinks are sold on every corner by street vendors in Sicily. They are extremely colourful, very fruity syrups mixed with freshly squeezed citrus juice and topped up with sparkling water.

If Palermo is a byword for street food, then Catania can boast the same for beverages, or "street drinks". At the heart of every *piazza principale*, unassuming and reserved, but colourfully stocked and ready for action, they stand on the pavement and wait. In a matter of seconds, out of nowhere, a crowd of people forms. This throng can disperse as quickly as it assembled. People don't linger for long, so everything needs to be done quickly. Swift service, dexterity, expertise, and great quality, all at incredibly low prices.

These institutions are originally from Catania. The name can seem a little unceremonious: *chiosco*. But these are far more than mere "kiosks". These little buildings, with their protruding roofs, are in fact vibrant street bars. The finest *chioschi* were built in the Liberty Style (Catania is not just a Baroque town, it also offers plenty of Art Nouveau delights) and are designed with a rectangular or octagonal floor plan. You may not be able to buy a newspaper here, but you will find the healthiest drink in the world. It is also the best-selling drink in summer. And it consists of just three natural ingredients, mixed together in a few swift steps by the vendor to create the renowned *seltz limone e sale*.

A bit of sea salt, two lemons (the juice squeezed by hand using a wonderful brass press, which is still manufactured by true master craftsmen), mixed with highly carbonated water that shoots out of a tap. That's all you need for this classic drink, made in Catania, and the queen of the *chioschi*. It is also non-alcoholic, like all the other popular drinks sold at *chioschi*, the ultimate outdoor meeting places for Catania's residents. Gaudy coloured syrups catch the eye, often stored in ornate glass bottles next to piles of oranges and lemons.

As well as *seltz limone e sale*, you can order the south Italian favourite *frappè* (fruit mixed with milk), your favourite *caffè*, *misto frutto* (puréed fruits combined with the ubiquitous soda), and drinks mixed with your choice of syrup. These can be made from tart red or green

mandarins, sweet pineapples, refreshing watermelons and oranges, astringent green bananas, strawberries, mint, *orzata* (almond syrup), or even tamarind. Depending on the *chiosco*, there may even be granita on offer.

The kiosks, known slightly confusingly as *o ciospu* in the Catanian dialect, evolved from the ancient occupation of the water vendor, the *acquaioli*. This street trader would sell drinking water on the street, which he had collected from a well or spring and transported in large terracotta containers to be offered to passers-by on market day, or at street festivals. Sometimes this would be flavoured with a dash of lemon juice in Catania. In Palermo, on the other hand, the *acquaioli* sold *acqua e zammù* (water with anise), which was a legacy of the Arab rulers.

Just as *seltz limone e sale* is quintessentially Catanian, the term "seltzer" is recognized around the world. The ancient Romans called sparkling, dancing water *aqua saltare*. The word *saltare* became *selters*, and now this term is used in many languages as the unofficial term for carbonated mineral water.

Some popular *chioschi* in Catania that are well worth a visit (particularly in the heat of summer):

Chiosco Sicilia Seltz
Corso Sicilia

Chiosco Giammona
Piazza Vittorio Emanuele III

Chiosco del Borgo
Piazza Cavour

Chiosco Stazione
Piazza Papa Giovanni XXIII

The last of these may not be the most fashionable *chiosco*, nor does it have the most elegant architecture, but the drinks here taste just that little bit better, maybe because this *chiosco* is one of very few to serve them in a glass rather than a plastic beaker.

Sparkling salted lemon drink, from Catania

Seltz limone e sale

250ml (9fl oz) chilled
  sparkling water
pinch of sea salt or sea
  salt flakes
4 tbsp freshly squeezed
  lemon juice, ideally from
  Sicilian *Verdelli* lemons
pinch of bicarbonate of soda

This is the ideal summer drink! In summer we naturally sweat more, and this cooling process also causes us to lose important minerals. These can be restored with a *seltz limone e sale.* You should use a 400ml (14fl oz) glass, as the bicarbonate of soda creates froth. This recipe can also be made beautifully using 10–20 per cent purified sea water, but, in that case, don't add any salt, just the bicarbonate of soda for the froth effect.

Pour 200ml (7fl oz) sparkling water into a glass. Stir in the salt until it dissolves. Add the lemon juice. Top up with the remaining sparkling water, stir in the bicarbonate of soda (careful, it froths up), and drink immediately.

A Sicilian gin fizz

Gino fizz

25ml (scant 1fl oz) dry gin
2 tsp sugar syrup
good pinch of sea salt or
  sea salt flakes
4 tsp freshly squeezed lemon
  juice, ideally from
  Sicilian *Verdelli* lemons
4–6 ice cubes
100ml (3$^{1}/_{2}$fl oz) sparkling
  water
broad strip of zest from
  1 organic lemon

To be honest, it is odd that the original gin fizz lacks salt. That's why I've included the Sicilian version here, where sea salt is essential!

Vigorously shake the gin, sugar syrup, sea salt, and lemon juice in a cocktail shaker with 2–3 ice cubes.

Pour through a fine sieve into a glass containing 2–3 ice cubes. Top up with sparkling water and garnish with the lemon zest, or place this in the cocktail itself. Cin-Gin!

Tip: Why not use a couple of long (and environmentally friendly) macaroni tubes as straws.

Almond milk with a hint of green lemon

Latte di mandorla al limone verde

100g (3¹/₂oz) almonds, roughly
   ground (ideally *Romana* or
   a blend of almonds from
   Noto, see p180)
sugar, to taste
zest from 1 organic lemon,
   ideally a Sicilian *Verdelli*
   lemon, white
   pith removed, or from
   1 organic lime

The process for making almond milk can either be complicated or straightforward. Concetto Scardaci (see p180) takes the simple approach. The almonds are processed including their brown skins, because these contain important nutrients. In summer, his family drinks nothing but this almond milk, so Concetto is engaged in constant production to keep up with demand! His habit of adding green lemon zest is inherited from his mother, and he uses the skin from the *Verdelli* lemon which is in season during the summer, to give the milk an additional freshness. If you prefer things less sweet, you don't need to add any sugar or other sweetener to this milk. In fact, reducing or avoiding sugar helps emphasize the flavour of the high-quality almonds. In the past, almond farmers would have made this drink from the nut scraps, the leftover bits that couldn't be sold. So an authentic version combines the flavours of several different varieties of almond.

Get 2 bowls ready. Pour into one of them 500ml (16fl oz) of water. Put half the almonds into the centre of a muslin cloth and twist it firmly to make a compact ball.

Submerge this in the water then remove and wring out over the second bowl until no more white almond liquid comes out. Put the cloth ball back in the water and repeat until the bowl with the water is empty.

Then pour another 500ml (16fl oz) of water into the empty bowl. Discard the used almond paste and put the remaining almonds into the cloth. Repeat the process.

Now sweeten the "milk" to taste, or just leave it as it is, with the lemon zest. Decant into a sterilized bottle with a screw-top lid.

Leave the flavours to develop for about 1 hour in the refrigerator. Discard the lemon zest before drinking. The almond milk will keep for about 3 days in the refrigerator.

A Sicilian aperitif

Aperitivo Siciliano

The *aperitivo* is not actually a Sicilian tradition. Sicilians don't go to a bar to drink alcohol, but rather to enjoy a *caffè* and possibly to eat something sweet (which may in fact contain alcohol). But these days the fashion for *aperitivos* has extended from the Italian mainland into Sicily. With their new-found self-confidence, Sicilians take a different approach to their northern compatriots. *Aperitivos* are sometimes (more and more frequently, in fact) served with local specialities, often with little snacks inspired by the island's ancient history.

Serves 4
Prep 25–35 mins

Prickly pear and pomegranate cocktail

Cocktail al fico d'India e melagrana

2 prickly pears
1 large pomegranate
16-20 ice cubes
120ml (4fl oz) Amaro liqueur
400ml (14fl oz) spumante wine, for instance Mon Pit Brut Rosé from Cantine Russo
zest from 1 organic lemon, divided into 4
4 large sage leaves
4 long rosemary sprigs

1–2 little bowls of *fave fritte* (see p143)
Mini sesame panini with lemon marmalade and scamorza (see p147)
1–2 little bowls of pickled lupini beans, or crisps, or peanuts

Peel the prickly pears (see p171) and purée the fruit. Discard the skins or fry them (see p171).

Halve the pomegranate and juice each section using a manual press. Alternatively, scoop out all the seeds, remove the white membrane and process the seeds in a juicer.

Put 4–5 ice cubes into each of 4 balloon glasses, pour over the prickly pear purée and stir in the pomegranate juice. Divide the Amaro between each glass, stir well and top up with spumante. Put a piece of lemon zest and a sage leaf into each glass and finish with a sprig of rosemary shaped in an arch (see photo, bottom), or simply inserted lengthways.

Serve with *fave fritte*, filled mini panini, and pickled lupini beans.

IL VINO

"Respect the earth and her equilibrium. Respect the vineyard by cultivating it wisely and farming sensitively. Respect the fermentation process by using indigenous yeasts. Respect the wine as if it was a person, bringing its own world, its own history, its own atmosphere."

Arianna Occhipinti

A renewed appreciation of native vine varieties will not only prevent them from disappearing, it will also enrich the world of wine in numerous different ways. This has recently been demonstrated with great success in Sicily with the grape variety Nero d'Avola. But that was only the beginning in terms of painstakingly transforming the island's vinicultural landscape.

Viniculture and wine making have left their mark on the regions around Mount Etna since ancient times. The vineyards benefit immensely from the special microclimate around Etna, and have been developed on small and medium terraces carved into the hillsides. Since 1968, the wines produced here – *bianco superiore, bianco, rosso,* and *rosato* – have been authorised to use the Etna DOC registered designation of origin. The Etna region encompasses 21 municipalities. The region's indigenous vines are Nerello Mascalese and Nerello Cappuccio (both red wine varieties), and Carricante and Minnella (both white wine varieties).

In addition to these varieties from Etna, Sicily's other important native grape varieties include Catarratto (white), Frappato (red), Grecanico (white), Grillo (white), Inzolia/Ansonica (white), Albanello (white), Alicante/Guarnaccia (red), Corinto (red), Damaschino (white), Malvasia di Lipari (white), Moscato bianco (white), Moscato d'Alessandria/Zibibbo (white), Nocera (red), and Perricone (red). There are also countless ancient varieties of vine, making up a seemingly endless list which has not yet been fully defined.

Over the last couple of years, a new and very welcome trend has emerged in the world of wine. Previously, global wine stocks consisted almost entirely of just a few varieties of vine, namely the "classic" French varieties such as Chardonnay, Cabernet Sauvignon, and Merlot. These are varieties that have gradually spread from France for use in wine production globally. But many regions have long since cultivated other, equally excellent, grapes for wine. These include a number of native Italian varieties, especially from the south of the country.

A special find from the time of the ancient Greeks shows just how far back Sicilian viniculture goes. The discovery was made at the archaeological site of Kamarina, located in the present-day province of Ragusa, and includes the depiction of a landscape full of vines. In fact, interestingly, it shows a woman running a wine business. Just 16km (10 miles) from Kamarina lies Vittoria. This is where Cerasuolo di Vittoria is produced, the only Sicilian wine to bear the DOCG seal (issued since 2005). And it is also home to the most successful vintner in the new generation of Sicilian winemakers. And, like her ancient ancestor nearby, she too is a woman.

Arianna Occhipinti was born in Trapani in 1982. Later the family moved to Vittoria, where her father worked as an architect. Her uncle, Giusto Occhipinti, founded Azienda Agricola COS in 1980, along with Giambattista Cilia and Cirino Strano. At that time, he already had extensive experience as a wine producer and today he manages one of the best wineries in Sicily.

Arianna's philosophy regarding wine and life goes even further: "My wine understands the land from which it comes. The wine I like to produce is not just an organic wine, it goes beyond merely complying with the countless EU regulations governing organic produce. Its most important characteristic is that it is a natural wine, and I like to see a similar natural essence in myself. My wine is inspired by my instinct for authenticity and by the importance I place on love. This is a wine that offers harmony and strength, that speaks volumes about its wonderful country of origin, and about me. That's why I'm absolutely convinced that natural wine is not just a good-quality wine, but also a humane wine."

At a young age, Arianna developed a strong and close relationship with her successful uncle and a particular affinity with his chosen profession. When she was 16, she accompanied him to Verona to the VinItaly wine fair, where she saw all the different wines on show and began to understand their cultural context and the many exceptional

people involved in this business. Her future path was immediately clear. She studied viniculture and oenology in Milan before returning to Sicily where, in 2004, she kicked off her career with a one-hectare (2.5-acre) vineyard, introducing her very first wine to the market at the age of just 22.

Today, Arianna owns almost 30 times this quantity of land, all of which is farmed organically, predominantly for the cultivation of two traditional grape varieties from Vittoria, Frappato and Nero d'Avola. These are used to produce the well-known Cerasuolo di Vittoria DOC, which consists of equal proportions of Nero d'Avola and Frappato. Arianna named the wine Grotte Alte.

Cerasuolo di Vittoria is a blend that has always been produced in Vittoria and was previously known as Rosso di Vittoria. The town of Vittoria was founded on 24 April 1607 by the eponymous Countess Vittoria Colonna Henriquez-Cabrera. She entrusted the first 75 settlers with a hectare

of land each, as long as they grew vines. So viniculture was in Vittoria's blood from the moment of its birth.

Before I leave Vittoria, I ask Arianna what her favourite dishes are. She has three: pasta with *bottarga di tonno*, pasta with garlic and wild fennel, and, top of the list, her mama's incredible *caponata*, which uses aubergines, almonds, some carrots, and celery. She can't give me the recipe, because even her mother hasn't been able to explain it in detail to her! But she can recommend a wine to go with it: SP68 Rosso. This involves a blend of 70 per cent Frappato and 30 per cent Nero d'Avola. But the name also evokes the Strada Provinciale 68, the main road that runs past Arianna's *azienda*!

Addresses

PROVINCE OF AGRIGENTO
Produce
Antichi Sapori
Amante Maria Antonia
Via Cesare Battisti 20
92100 Agrigento
(with product tastings)

Accommodation
Camere a Sud
Elvira Mangione
Via Ficani 6
92100 Agrigento
www.camereasud.it

Eating out
Siculò
Via Pirandello 21
92100 Agrigento

Ninin Osteria
Via Ficani 32
92100 Agrigento

Ristorante La Madia
Pino Cuttaia
Corso F. Re Capriata 22
92027 Licata
(2 Michelin stars)
www.ristorantelamadia.it

PROVINCE OF CALTANISSETTA
Ice cream
Maestri gelatieri
Il Bignè
Nicola Antonio Salerno
Via Calabria 66
93100 Caltanissetta

PROVINCE OF CATANIA
Produce
Giuseppe Camuglia
Azienda Casearia Camuglia S.r.l.
Via Federico II 105
95012 Castiglione di Sicilia
(cheese)
www.alcantaraformaggi.it

Nunzio Caruso
Azienda Acquavena
Contrada Acquavena
95034 Bronte

(Capra Argentata dell'Etna)
www.sicilianroots.com/eng/produttori/
azienda-acquavena

Nino Testa
Testa Conserve
Via Testa 23
95126 Catania
(canned fish)
www.testaconserve.it

Cantine Russo S.r.l.
Via Corvo (SP64) Solicchiata
95012 Castiglione di Sicilia
(wine)
www.cantinerusso.eu

Eating out
Me Cumpari Turiddu
Piazza Turi Ferro 36/38
95131 Catania
www.mecumparituriddu.it

Bar Pasticceria Savia
Via Etnea
95100 Catania
www.savia.it

Bar Pasticceria Spinella
Via Etnea 292
95131 Catania
www.pasticceriaspinella.it

Pasticceria Ricca
Via Risorgimento 35
95040 Ramacca
(you must try: cannoli with
artichoke cream)

Via Santa Filomena
95129 Catania
(street packed with youthful,
new eateries)

Chioschi di Catania
Chiosco Sicilia Seltz
Corso Sicilia

Chiosco Giammona
Piazza V. Emanuele III

Chiosco del Borgo
Piazza Cavour

Chiosco Stazione
Piazza Papa Giovanni XXIII

Information
Chiara La Spina
City Guide Catania
www.instagram.com/chiaralsp

PROVINCE OF ENNA
Produce
Dott. Angelo Calì Contrada Rossi
94013 Leonforte
(fava larga, black pulses)
www.leonforteagricola.it

Mitèra – Azienda agricola Prestifilippo
Alex Prestifilippo
Via Bellini 16
94013 Leonforte
(fava larga, black pulses)
www.mitera.it

SeminiAmo
Famiglia Amore
Viale Signore Ritrovato
94012 Barrafranca
(ancient grain varieties and
bronze-die pasta)
www.seminiamo.com

PROVINCE OF MESSINA
Produce
Salvatore Romano and Karin Meier
Tasting Sicily
Via Vittorio Veneto 10
98056 Graniti
www.vitasicula.com

Azienda Agricola Marchetta Malvasia
delle Lipari
Via Umberto I 9
98050 Malfa
(capers and wine from Salina)
www.vinidisalina.it

Cantine Colosi
Via Nazionale 80
98050 Malfa
(wine)
www.cantinecolosi.it

Accommodation
Hotel & Ristorante Signum
Via Scalo 15
98050 Malfa
www.hotelsignum.it
(The restaurant is run by
Italy's latest star chef
Martina Caruso.)

Case Vacanza Cafarella
Via Scalo 10
98050 Malfa
www.casecafarella.it

Eating out
Da Alfredo Via Marina Garibaldi
98050 Lingua
(pane cunzato)

Trattoria A Quadara
Via Roma 88
98050 Malfa
www.aquadaratrattoria.it

Gastronomia Rundo
Via Risorgimento 150
98050 Santa Marina Salina
(cannoli with capers)

Bars
In Sé Natura
Via Nuova Indipendenza 7
98050 Malfa

Saretto Bambara
Bam Bar
Via di Giovanni 43
98039 Taormina

Bar Malvasia
Via Roma 33
98050 Malfa

PA. PE. RO'
Strada Provinciale 182
98050 Rinella

Information
Valeria La Spina
City Guide Taormina
www.instagram.com/valeria_laspina

PROVINCE OF PALERMO
Produce
G. Formaggi
Corso C. Finocchiaro Aprile 129
90138 Palermo

Bar
Ideal Caffè Stagnitta
Discesa dei Giudici 42
90133 Palermo
www.idealcaffe.it
(traditional coffee roasting house
and bar)

Street food
Giorgio Flaccavento
www.palermostreetfood.com

Vucciria
Piazza Caracciolo
90133 Palermo

Mercato di Ballarò
Via Ballaro, 1
90134 Palermo

Mayor
Leoluca Orlando
Palazzo delle Aquile
Piazza Pretoria 1
90133 Palermo
(mayor of Palermo,
the capital of Sicily)

PROVINCE OF RAGUSA
Produce
Frantoi Cutrera
Maria, Giusy, Salvatore Cutrera
Contrada Piano D'Acqua 71
97012 Chiaramonte Gulfi
(olive oil)
www.frantoicutrera.it

Azienda Agricola Arianna
Occhipinti
Arianna Occhipinti
SP68 Vittoria-Pedalino KM 3.3
97019 Vittoria
(wine)
www.agricolaocchipinti.it

Accommodation
Neropece suites
Signora Rita
Via Capitano Bocchieri 52
97100 Ragusa

Eating out
Duomo
Ciccio Sultano
Via Capitano Bocchieri 31
97100 Ragusa
(2 Michelin stars)
www.cicciosultano.it

I Banchi
Peppe Cannistrà, Ciccio Sultano
Via Orfanotrofio 39
97100 Ragusa
www.ibanchiragusa.it

PROVINCE OF SYRACUSE
Produce
Concetto Scardaci
Via Littara 11
96017 Noto
(almonds)

Cantine Gulino
Via Daniele Impellizzeri 29
96100 Fanusa
(wine)
www.cantinegulino.it

Eating out
Ristorante Crocifisso
Via Principe Umberto 46
96017 Noto
www.ristorantecrocifisso.it

Caffè Sicilia
Corrado Assenza
Corso Vittorio Emanuele 125
96017 Noto

I Rizzari
Via Libertà 63
96011 Augusta

Osteria Sveva
Piazza Federico di Svevia 1
96100 Siracusa

PROVINCE OF TRAPANI
Produce
Molini del Ponte
Via G. Parini 29
91022 Castelvetrano
(ancient grain varieties and olive oil)
www.molinidelponte.com

Eating out
Pasticceria Maria Grammatico
Via Vittorio Emanuele 14
91100 Erice
www.mariagrammatico.it

Maestri gelatieri
Gelateria Liparoti
Maurizio Liparoti
Viale delle Sirene 21
91100 Trapani

Euro Bar Dattilo
Via Giuseppe Garibaldi 11–13
91027 Dattilo
(the best cannoli in the world)

Index

ACKNOWLEDGMENTS

DK would like to thank Arani Sinha, Tanya Singhal, and Rishi Bryan for editorial assistance, and Vanessa Bird for indexing.

PICTURE CREDITS
All images supplied by Cettina Vicenzino, except:
Cover: Grapes 123RF.com/lachris77, background Pixabay/Predra6_Photos
Murales (Streetart): page 10 Zay, page 13 Rosk and Loste, page 17 Tannis Hopkins, page 154 Lelea Byron

GRAZZI ASSAI!

…to all these beautiful Sicilians: Famigghia Amore, Ciccio Sultano, Gabriella Cicero, Peppe Cannistrà, Raul Pace, Jessica Carpin, Carmelo Cilia, Paolo Moltisanti, Elvira Mangione, Geta Eris, Salvatore Romano, Karin Meier, Maria Grammatico, Giuseppe Camuglia, Nunzio Caruso, Nino Testa, Gaetano Marchetta, Angelo Calì, Alessandro Vezzosi, Giammona brothers, Alfredo Oliveri, Rosario Bambara, Arianna Occhipinti, Pietro Colosi I.–III., Lidia Labate, Vincenzo Russo, Ricardo Pace, Giorgio Flaccavento, Leoluca Orlando, Corrado Assenza, Concetto Scardaci, signuri Gioè and all the people of the Cape, Baddarò and Vuccirìa to Palermu and chiddi da Piscarìa to Catania.

…to the team at Dorling Kindersley: Monika Schlitzer for trusting in me and giving me so much freedom to fulfil this island dream; Annemarie Heinel for providing the best support you could ever wish for, and for the good fortune which lead to another treasured book collaboration; Sibylle Schug and Barbara Mally for the wonderful design work; Annika Genning for her skilled editorial work on my text. Grazzi assai!

…to my family: Maria, Joachim, Pina, Valeria, Chiara, Santo. Grazzi, grazzi assai!

For DK UK

Translator Alison Tunley
Editors Amy Slack, Dawn Titmus
Editorial assistant Millie Andrew
Senior art editor Glenda Fisher
Jacket designer Ella Egidy
Jacket co-ordinator Lucy Philpott
Producer, pre-production Heather Blagden
Producer Rebecca Parton
Managing editor Stephanie Farrow
Managing art editor Christine Keilty

For DK Delhi

DTP Designer Umesh Singh Rawat
Pre-production Manager Sunil Sharma

For DK Germany

Recipes, text, photography Cettina Vicenzino
Editorial Annika Genning
Internal design, typography, implementation Sibylle Schug, Barbara Mally
Programme management Monika Schlitzer
Editorial management and project support Anne Heinel
Production manager Dorothee Whittaker
Production controller Ksenia Lebedeva
Production Claudia Bürgers

First British edition 2020
Dorling Kindersley Limited
80 Strand, London, WC2R 0RL

A CIP catalogue record for this book
is available from the British Library.
ISBN: 978-0-2414-1260-2

Printed and bound in China

A WORLD OF IDEAS:
SEE ALL THERE IS TO KNOW

www.dk.com